75 GREAT HIKES

in and near

PALM SPRINGS

and the

COACHELLA VALLEY

*Philip Ferranti, Bruce Hagerman and
Denice Hagerman*

Photographs by Authors Except as Noted

KENDALL/HUNT PUBLISHING COMPANY
4050 Westmark Drive   Dubuque, Iowa 52002

TABLE OF CONTENTS

SAN JACINTO MOUNTAINS

SANTA ROSA MOUNTAINS

JOSHUA TREE NATIONAL PARK

SAN GORGONIO PASS AND NEARBY

ACKNOWLEDGMENTS

From Philip
Special thanks to Les and Shirley Larson for first introducing me to the local trails.

From Bruce & Denice
The following wonderful friends hiked and explored the trails with us, making our trips even more wonderful: Roger & Maria Keezer, Ray Wilson, Sue Bobek, Bob & June Kuhnau and Jeff St. Thomas.

Much appreciation to all the hike leaders and support volunteers in the Coachella Valley Hiking Club for sharing the joy of hiking these magnificent trails.

Special thanks and praise goes to Sue Bobek for her wonderful photos.

The authors wish to acknowledge the tremendous contributions made by the Desert Trail Riders and the Coachella Valley Trails Council for their on-going efforts to build, maintain and protect the many beautiful trails in and near the Coachella Valley.

INTRODUCTION

THE TOPOGRAPHY

This hiking guide takes you into the interior of Southern California, where mountains slope down into deserts and reach out into canyons and the surrounding low foothills to form the 60 mile stretch of land known as the Coachella Valley. The San Andreas Fault cuts through this valley, contributing to its formation while causing those infamous earthquakes.

The northwest of the Coachella Valley is bordered by the San Bernardino Mountains, with Southern California's tallest peak, San Gorgonio (11,501 feet) acting as a sentinel guarding the San Gorgonio Pass that ushers visitors into the valley from the west.

The southwestern to west boundary of the valley is marked by the towering San Jacinto Mountain Range and San Jacinto Mountain, whose 10,800 foot massif fills the whole western skyline above Palm Springs. These same mountains provide the granite bedrock upon which the Desert Divide Ridge has been married to the Pacific Crest Trail (PCT), allowing hikers to traverse the entire 60 mile length of the mountains above the valley, all the way to Idyllwild, past San Jacinto Mountain and eventually across the Pass to the awaiting San Bernardino Mountains.

Looking south by southeast, one sees the Santa Rosa Mountains, with the twin peaks of Santa Rosa and Toro, dominating the horizon above La Quinta and Palm Desert. Lesser foothills carve their way along the valley floor to enfold the cities of Rancho Mirage, Cathedral City and the eastern side of Palm Springs.

To the north, the Little San Bernardino Mountains, Indio and Mecca Hills, Cottonwood and Orocopia Mountains complete the border of the Coachella Valley and provide an abundant number of canyons and interesting geological formations for hikers to explore.

Both the Santa Rosa and San Jacinto Mountains are relatively new, perhaps 20 million years old. They were formed when the Pacific Plate began to push against and into the North American Plate, causing forces deep within the earth's crust to uplift these ranges, while dredging up 500 million year old rocks to cover their slopes as granite boulders and sharp escarpments.

Across the valley, along the Mecca Hills, the San Andreas Fault has contributed to the valley formation by pulling the floor away from the southern mountains, thereby widening it and acting as a receptacle for the sand deposited from eroding granite and quartz rocks on the surrounding mountains.

Thus, within 70 miles of Palm Springs, more then a dozen mountain ranges and foothills provide the raw material for 750 miles of hiking trails, making this area one of the premier winter hiking destinations in the United States.

CLIMATE and WEATHER

The Coachella Valley represents the furthest reaches of the Colorado Desert. The mountains to the west that surround the valley, effectively block Pacific storms from unleashing their full potential. Annual rainfall amounts may reach 3 to 5 inches, while Los Angles is receiving 15 to 25 inches. Hikers need to respect the desert conditions in planning where and at what altitude they will hike, as well as when. What begins as a comfortable 70 degree sunrise hike, might end at 100 degrees plus by late afternoon.

Usually hikers can begin doing comfortable day hikes on the valley floor and in the lower foothills by November. The moderate temperatures allow hikes up to 6,000 feet all winter long, with only scattered, thin snow conditions at worse. By April, hikes should be planned for the higher elevations only. Short sunrise hikes on the desert floor and in the mountain canyons lasting until morning heat sets in can be safely done until late spring.

From June to mid-October, all the 6,000 to 10,000 foot elevation hikes are comfortably done. Sometimes during the dead of summer, when the Coachella Valley experiences 110 degree days, hikers can enjoy the many hikes along the PCT, and the Desert Divide Ridge overlooking the valley, in 70 degree weather . . . providing there is a cool, onshore Pacific breeze blowing, and the marine layer has penetrated inland from the coast.

In the Idyllwild-San Jacinto Mountain region, summer storms can suddenly gather and deliver a cold rain or even hail upon unprepared hikers. It is always wise to check the local forecast for what weather might be affecting the bay's hike. Still, the combination of mountains adjacent to deserts allow year-round hiking within 70 miles of the Coachella Valley, with the simple rule of thumb being "as temperatures rise, climb to higher elevations to hike."

FLORA and FAUNA

The Coachella Valley and nearby mountains reward the hiker with a generous diversity of plant and animal life. Dozens of cactus species, yucca, ocotillo, sage, smoketree, and desert flowers sweep up from the valley floor to the surrounding foothills and join with ribbonwood, manzanita, juniper, and scrub oak. They, in turn, eventually encounter pine, fir, cedar, and oak that blanket the mountains and give an incredibly distinct and fragrant "desert-mountain" scent, unique to this area.

Bighorn sheep, coyotes, golden eagles, red-tailed hawks, rabbit, deer and even mountain lion are just a few of the animals found along our trails. Visits to the Living Desert and the Palm Springs Desert Museum yield a rich educational experience for anyone wanting to learn about the local plant and animal life.

USING THIS BOOK

At the top of each hike is found useful information for planning your hike. This mini-guide includes:

- Length: always given in round trip mileage or one-way (if a shuttle is indicated it is done so in the text).

- Season: means the best time of year to hike a given trail in relative comfort (please understand, however, that desert hiking is an iffy proposition, in that we have seen 95 degree temperatures in February and 70 degrees in April! A good precaution during the obvious warmer months is to start "early," thereby avoiding the possible surge in temperatures by mid-afternoon).

- Hiking Time: is an estimate based on a 2 to 2.5 mph pace with some time given for breaks and lunch. We have found that going uphill takes at least 25% longer than going downhill. This calculation is included in estimated times. Note that most hikes in this guide end by going downhill.

- Information: involves the agency where you can get maps, guide books and advice on your hike, with current phone numbers of that agency . . . BLM (Bureau of Land Management), USDA Forest Service, Joshua Tree National Park. The new California Desert Protection Act of 1994 affects your access and use of BLM land. Consult with the BLM agency in Palm Springs for additional information.

- Elevation Gain/Loss: is measured from the beginning of the hike to the end, including return. Hikers need to know their own stamina and endurance, aerobic conditioning levels and the like, before attempting any hike, especially the strenuous ones.
- Difficulty: is a relative term, but considers all of the above factors.

The Coachella Valley Hiking Club standards are used in this book as follows:

- Easy . . . up to 500 feet elevation gain and up to 6 miles in length.
- Moderate . . . between 500 to 1,800 feet elevation gain and between 6 to 10 miles in length.
- Strenuous . . . over 1,800 feet elevation gain, and between 8 to 15 miles in length, or longer.

All hikes in this book are "day hikes," but many can be taken over several days if the hiker wishes to camp out.

Some trails are deceptive in their demands. A hike of 6 miles in length is usually considered easy, but when most of the elevation gain comes during the return portion's last 2 miles, it might be done as a moderate hike. On some hikes the strenuous portion comes all at the very beginning, while the remaining 80% is moderate or even easy, i.e. the Zen Center Trail. Some hikers find steep downhill sections more difficult than uphill, because of knee or toe stress.

SAFETY

Desert hiking requires more safety than a casual walk along a National Park trail. Water is essential to survival, and no hiker knows what events await on the trail. We suggest carrying at least 2 quarts of cool water for hikes up to 6 miles and more water for longer distances. During the hot season you might try freezing 50% of your drink, i.e. Gatorade, a sport drink etc., then adding the remainder of cool liquid the morning of the hike. This ensures a cool drink all day!

Protect your head with a hat of some sort, use sunscreen, carry extra food and water, sunglasses, wind breaker for the higher elevations, basic first aid essentials like aspirin, tweezers, bandaids, moleskin and anything else you feel supports your personal safety. Carry a comb in case you brush against a cholla cactus . . . glide the comb down through the thorns and flick off the entire ball of cactus.

The beauty of these areas demand respect. If you pack it in . . . pack it out!

A map of the area where you are hiking is always a good idea, with a compass to assist in land navigation. The CV Trails Council with the BLM has published a good trail map of the area. Other hiking equipment can be had from Hal at his Great Outdoors hiking & camping shop on Hwy 111 in Palm Desert (773-4880).

It's a good idea to hike **WITH SOMEONE ELSE**! In case of injury, you get lost, etc., two, three or more hikers are better than one. Let someone know where you are going and when you expect to return. The Coachella Valley Hiking Club, (619) 345-6234, conducts guided hikes all year long and has hiked every trail mentioned in this book. Give them a call for information and perhaps accompany them on a hike as a guest.

Wild animals present little hazard. Snake bites are best avoided by looking carefully around where you intend to sit, rest or eat, making sure not to put your hand under logs, rocks and bushes. Wearing long pants is another protection against snake bites, as they might hit you in a strike, but be unable to get clean leverage and angle to pierce your pant material. Mountain lions have been observed in the desert and mountains nearby, but again, traveling in numbers almost insures that no harm will befall you.

During the summer months hiking at higher elevations can be quite pleasant, with temperatures reaching into the low 80's. In August and early September, however, summer storms can blow up quickly over the mountains. Rain gear and a warm long-sleeved light jacket will prove ample protection.

Hiking equipment: wide brimmed hat, long sleeve shirt, pants, day pack, walking stick, and sturdy boots

THE COACHELLA VALLEY HIKING CLUB (CVHC)

In October of 1992, the Coachella Valley Hiking Club was formed with the purpose of organizing hikes into the magnificent deserts and mountains surrounding the Coachella Valley, and educating the public as to the availability and nature of the great hiking trails found there. Visitors are welcomed as guests for a day hike and information is readily available by calling their number (619) 345-6234. This club is very active and sponsors over 300 hikes per year.

A HIKING PHILOSOPHY

Hiking is what our ancestors did effortlessly as part of their daily routine. Hunting, migrating to new pastures, warmer climates and homelands is part of the psyche of human beings. We feel "home" where nature draws us into her beautiful deserts, mountains, canyons, prairie, along sea shores, lakes and rivers, under star-canopied skies . . . wherever the plant and animal kingdoms engage the nurturing earth.

The advent of civilization greatly impacted our commune with nature. Cities enclosed us. Still the call of the wild is meant for all people, a beckoning to primeval stirrings, and the peace of the quiet beauty of the land. Hiking is our entree into the nurturing enfolds of nature. We shed the stresses, onslaughts of media encroachments, demands and noise of "civilization" when we hike "out into nature" and release their demanding grip on our longing hearts and spirits.

Hiking is best approached as a way of life, a creative lifestyle, part of the daily fabric of existence. To walk each day, somewhere touched by nature's gentle hand, to hike each week into the calming embrace of nature . . . this is a goal worthy of those pursuing a good quality of life. Trails are like a collection of recipes that only nourish when acted on . . . they are meant to be walked, not merely acknowledged.

The rewards are great. A moderate hike burns almost 400 calories per hour. Six hours on the trail goes a long way towards firming, toning, and weight reduction. Hiking rejuvenates and energizes the hiker, mentally, emotionally, physically and spiritually. It offers us the needed beauty of nature, teaches us her quiet lessons and reminds us that there awaits a shelter from any of life's storms.

Hiking is a metaphor for life itself . . . we climb our inner mountains and seek quiet meadows within our souls, following whatever guide proves worthy of our allegiance. Unlike so many modern activities, a day on the trail has a set beginning, middle and end . . . by trail's end we accomplish something of real value while participating in an activity free from pretense, contrivance and bravado. Hiking is honest.

Along the trail we can share something of ourselves with our fellow travelers. The community of Man is built on small but precious sharing such as takes place while on a hike.

This book is therefore an open invitation to visit those unique, beautiful desert, canyon and mountain trails in and nearby this Coachella Valley. Ask any hiker who has been there, "What is out there?" Come see for yourself. Come reach beyond your daily routine and . . . enjoy!

> **"If you pick 'em up, O Lord,**
> **I'll put 'em down."**
>
> Anon.
> *The Prayer of the Tired Walker*

MECCA HILLS

1 THE PAINTED CANYON/ LADDER CANYON LOOP

Length: 5 miles
Hiking Time: 3–4 hours
Elevation Gain: 500 feet
Difficulty: Easy

Season: October to April
Information: BLM Office
Palm Springs
(619) 251-4800

At the northeast corner of southern California's inland Coachella Valley lies a confluence of several earthquake faults, including the well-known San Andreas fault. Here the land is uplifted, contorted and compressed into wild shapes resembling the mountains of the moon. Complementing this geological upheaval is an explosion of vibrant colors formed by the presence of minerals from deep within the earth's crust. This entire exotic land has been designated a wilderness area and is known as the Mecca Hills. At the heart of this twisted land is spectacular Painted Canyon, so named because of the profusion of colorful mineral rock deposits. This canyon is further accented by the Ladder Canyon loop hike, which treats the hiker to slot canyons, magnificent vistas of the Coachella Valley and finally an incredible geological adventure into the interior of Painted Canyon.

DIRECTIONS: To reach Painted Canyon, take I-10 to the Mecca Hwy 111 expressway, which is four miles east of Indio. Take the expressway until it ends, turn right until you reach the stoplight, make a left and proceed 6 miles until you reach the town of Mecca. Turn left into Mecca. You will now be on Hwy 195, which you will take out of town approximately 5 miles, cross the canal and go another .25 mile. On the right is the sign for Painted Canyon. Turn left and travel 4 miles on this improved dirt road until it dead ends into a turnaround and park. A regular automobile can travel this road but a 4WD is recommended. Check with the BLM office in Palm Springs for road conditions.

Hike the wide-mouthed canyon to the east or right of the road sign, not the canyon beyond the end of the road sign, for about .25 mile until you see the metal post on your right. Left of this post, just across the canyon, is the entrance to Ladder Canyon, hidden somewhat by the boulder slide. Travel up and to the right of the slide and you will come to the first of several ladders. This ladder will take you into a long slot canyon from which you gradually ascend. Stay to the right until you see the switchbacks climbing the hill to your right. This will be at least .25 mile from the first ladder. This switchback trail leads to another trail at the top of the hill. Continue left or north along the ridge for the next mile plus. You will be treated to spectacular vistas of the Coachella Valley, the Mecca Hills, Salton Sea and the surrounding Santa Rosa, San Jacinto, Cottonwood and Orocopia Mountains. The ridge trail takes you above Painted Canyon until you drop down into it and start your return loop by heading south, down canyon.

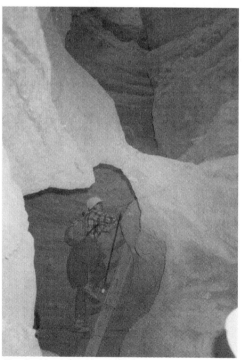

First Ladder in Ladder Canyon
Photo by Sue Bobek

This return trip is highlighted by colorful mineral rock formations of red, purple, green, dusty rose, and countless other shades formed by the iron oxidation throughout the canyon. Stay right as you continue down canyon until you reach a narrow, enclosed section where one final ladder helps your descent onto the canyon floor. From this spot it's less than 1 mile back to your vehicle. This hike is best done with clear skies and bright sunshine, as the color of these canyons must be seen at their best to maximize the enjoyment of this spectacular hike.

Gateway to Ladder Canyon
Photo by Sue Bobek

Descending the last ladder
Photo by Sue Bobek

2 BOX CANYON'S CAVE HIKE "THE GROTTOS"

Length: 5 miles
Hiking Time: 3–4 hours
Elevation Gain: 300 feet
Difficulty: Moderate

Season: October to April
Information: BLM Office
Palm Springs
(619) 251-4800

At the eastern flank of the Mecca Hills Wilderness area lies Box Canyon. Within this upheaval of sandstone, mud hills and washes are two "cave" systems formed when an ancient river cut through sandstone mountains and earthquakes forced the collapse of part of these mountain systems to buttress against each other at their tops, leaving the bottom hollow or cave-like in appearance. The hike to the caves offers the hiker a stunning view of the Salton Sea and lower Coachella Valley mountain systems, suggesting Lower Baja California's Sea of Cortez.

DIRECTIONS: To reach this trailhead, known as the Sheep Hole Oasis Trail, follow the directions for the Painted Canyon hike as far as the sign to Painted Canyon. Continue past the sign, staying on Box Canyon Road (Hwy 195) exactly 5 miles until you see a red painted rock on the right shoulder. Pull off there onto the dirt road (jeep tracks) for about 100 yards until you reach the trailhead.

The trail begins in the sandy wash in back of the sign and quickly winds up and through mud-like hills. You are soon surprised at the top by a series of expansive vistas of the Salton Sea and lower Coachella Valley. As you proceed down the backside of the hills, you will see to your left and down in the wash several palm trees. At the base of these is a man-made water hole for the bighorn sheep known as Sheep Hole Oasis. This oasis serves as the chief source of water for the bighorns in the Box Canyon area.

When you reach the bottom of the hill, turn right into the wash for several hundred yards until you arrive at the larger wash. Make a left down the canyon, staying to your right along the canyon walls for shade and to examine the clay formations found in the hills. You eventually reach an iron gate which allows hikers to freely pass further into the canyon. A few hundred yards into this canyon brings you to a small canyon entrance to your left. Make this short side trip of .25 mile to view Hidden Springs Oasis. After returning to the main canyon, continue left to the first large canyon you come to. By following this canyon you finally reach the first cave system known as the "Grottos."

Climb up and to the right of the large blocked entrance and negotiate your way through a series of several cave systems. Bring a good flashlight, as the Grottos can be in complete darkness at several places. Pay close attention to rock overhangs and loose soil. I've taken many people through these caves, even small children, but some folks get spooked by the confines and darkness. You can continue for .5 mile through the length of the entire system and turn back after reaching the upper ends of the canyon.

When you retrace your route back to the main canyon, turn left and continue for another .75 mile until the canyon dead ends. There, to the left, is the entrance to the second "Grotto" cave. This system requires more caution, a lot of crawling and slow climbing up to the top, and surely necessitates a good flashlight. Hike this cave with at least one other person, but the more the merrier!

When you reach the top you can explore the ridges but you will find no trail. Return back the way you came. Note especially well where the canyon turns are. If you miss the last turn, marked by the rock colors, you will find yourself miles down canyon before you know it. This is a fun hike and filled with fantastic rock structures throughout both cave systems.

The Mecca Hills along "The Grottos" Trail
Photo by Sue Bobek

Coachella Valley Mountains from the trail

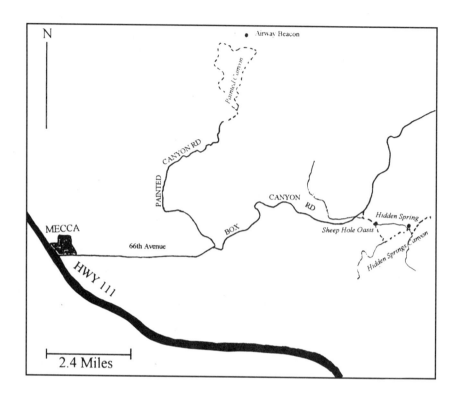

COACHELLA PRESERVE

3 THE PUSHAWALLA PALMS and CANYON TRAIL

Length: 6 miles
Hiking Time: 4 hours
Elevation Gain: 300 feet
Difficulty: Easy

Season: October to April
Information: Coachella Valley
Preserve
Thousand Palms
(619) 343-1234

The Coachella Valley Preserve

The 13,000 acre Coachella Valley Preserve is a lush concentration of California fan palms, rising miraculously in the alluvial gravel and sand deposits south of the Little San Bernardino Mountains and Indio Hills. The San Andreas Fault encourages water to seep up to the surface. Here seeds of the fan palm, nourished by this once subterranean water, have grown into more than 1,200 palms. A system of trails has been built to assist the visitor in seeing the wondrous effects of water and plant life surrounded by desert sands, low hills and gentle canyons.

> **DIRECTIONS:** To reach the Preserve, drive on I-10 to Washington Street, exit and drive left (north) for 5 miles reaching Thousand Palms Canyon Road. Turn right and park in the Preserve, located 2 miles after the turn.

To begin the Pushawalla Palms Trail, head southeast from the parking lot towards the rocky bluff across the road.

Once up the hill you are atop Bee-Rock Mesa. A trail heads to the left and takes you above Horseshoe Palms and then on into Pushawalla Palms Canyon. Or you can hike in a more southeast direction to arrive at the canyon before dropping down to explore the full length of the oasis.

Pushawalla Palms represents a long grove of palms growing in the narrow Pushawalla Canyon. There is a small stream running during the winter if rains have been plentiful. Anytime after March might be too hot for the unseasoned desert visitor to enjoy this hike, unless this hike is done in early morning.

Pushawalla Palms Oasis

Canyon Trail

4 WILLIS PALMS and WEST MESA TRAIL

Length: 3 miles
Hiking Time: 2 hours
Elevation Gain: 300 feet
Difficulty: Easy

Season: October to April
Information: Coachella Valley
Preserve
Thousand Palms
(619) 343-1234

This is another Coachella Valley Preserve hike that takes you to a grove of California fan palms situated on the San Andreas Fault and offers you expansive views of the western half of the Coachella Valley. While rated an easy hike, there is a climb up a short but steep cliff and hikers new to the desert should be aware of warmer springtime temperatures.

DIRECTIONS: To reach the trailhead, follow Washington Street north from I-10, as given in the directions for Pushawalla Palms Trail. After turning right at Thousand Palms Canyon Road look to your left at the low rise of hills. The trail begins after turning onto this road and is found to your left.

The trail starts west for .25 mile then north up a sandy wash. Stay right in the wash, follow the trail for another mile, then up the side of the cliff. You will see some great views of the western Coachella Valley. Continue following the trail as it turns south and back to your starting position. Always bring plenty of cool water on even a short desert hike such as this.

Willis Palms

Trail sign at the Coachella Valley Preserve

5 COACHELLA VALLEY PRESERVE TRAILS

Length: 6 miles
Hiking Time: 5 hours
Elevation Gain: 100 feet
Difficulty: Easy

Season: October to April
Information: Coachella Valley
Preserve
Thousand Palms
(619) 343-1234

The Coachella Valley Preserve is a great place to walk trails that are less demanding yet offer a real desert and oasis experience. The Preserve is truly an island in the desert, with generous plant and bird life surrounded by small desert canyons, hills, washes and mesas.

DIRECTIONS: The Preserve is reached by exiting from I-10 onto Washington Street, traveling north for 5 miles then right at Thousand Palms Road for 2 miles until you can see the lush vegetation on your left and the sign indicating the entrance.

There are several easy trails on the Preserve, ranging from less than .25 mile, 1, 1.4 and 3 miles. The elevation gain is less than 100 feet but the hikes do cover sandy trails, especially the Wash Trail, and tend to slow the hike into a gentle walk.

The Coachella Valley Preserve is indeed a place to walk, enjoy scenes of rich plant and bird life and capture the essence of a desert oasis. It is open from sunrise to sunset.

An oasis formed along the San Andreas Fault
Photo by
Sue Bobek

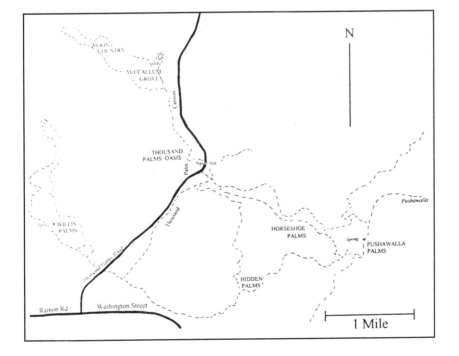

DESERT CITIES

6 GUADALUPE TRAIL to SUGARLOAF CAFE

Length: 15 miles
Hiking Time: 8 hours
Elevation Gain: 5,000 feet
Difficulty: Very Strenuous

Season: October to April
Information: BLM Office
Palm Springs
(619) 251-4800

While not commonly found on most hiking maps, the Guadalupe Trail to Sugarloaf Cafe is one of the premier strenuous, wilderness hikes in the Santa Rosa Mountains. This hike requires a shuttle, with cars parked at Sugarloaf Cafe on Hwy 74, 14 miles up the road from Palm Desert, and at the Boo Hoff/La Quinta trailhead. The climb up the northwest flank of Martinez Mountain, or at least close enough to be considered Martinez Mountain, gives hikers incredible vistas of the entire lower Coachella Valley and Salton Sea Basin. Eventually the trail penetrates the upper reaches of the Santa Rosa Wilderness and joins with the Cactus Spring Trail for the trek back through Horsethief Creek.

DIRECTIONS: To reach the trailhead, take Hwy 111 to La Quinta, turning south onto Washington Street until turning west (right) at Avenue 52. At Bermudas turn left, as it soon becomes Calle Tecate. Park on the south side of the road west of the water tank.

Start the hike by heading south of the parking lot, across the open flatlands of the water district to the cement dike, down across a field of small bushes, up the wash between the low mountains. Stay to the right. As the wash narrows, to the right you will see the Boo Hoff sign post, about 1 mile from the start.

From here, the hike is part of the Boo Hoff Trail, as it climbs steeply up the mountainside. At 3 miles up on your right is a small rock cairn, the "official" start of the Guadalupe Trail. This is actually an old Indian trail, which travels through the Guadalupe Canyon and on the rim of

Devil's Canyon. The trail looks onto steep, granite sanctuaries for big-horn sheep. Ahead of you as you climb south up this steep, rocky and sometimes faint trail, will be of a teepee type peak.

Further up the trail, 4 miles from the parked vehicles, is an Indian flat area (teepee type peak is now 50 feet east), where pottery pieces might be found. As the trail winds relentlessly up the mountains you reach a top area where pine and juniper begin to accent the slopes. As you enter the level mountainous area, you come upon an old "cowboy" camp, where the remains of stoves, iron implements, tin cans, etc. can be found strewn over a wide area. The trail pushes back from here into a dense canyon thicket, where a stream sometimes flows during wet winters. Eventually the trail breaks out into a widening wash, which you favor as it veers slowly to the right. In a short time you come to your first sign post, indicating that you are joined with the Cactus Spring Trail. Follow this trail right (west) for 2 miles to Horsethief Creek and another 2.5 miles to the Cactus Spring Trailhead. From here you can follow the jeep road to Sugarloaf Cafe just up the hill, along Hwy 74. As demanding as this trail is, it is worth all the effort . . . but is most safely done with someone knowing the way.

La Quinta, taken from on the way up to the Guadalupe Trail

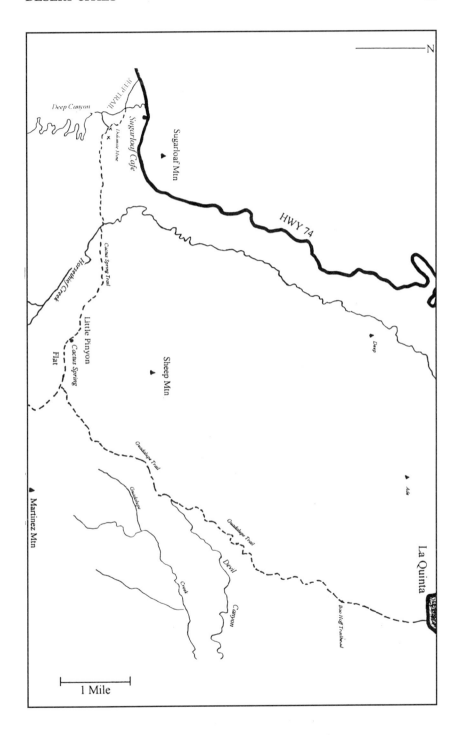

7 THE BOO HOFF TRAIL to LA QUINTA

Length: 12 miles   **Season:** October to April
Hiking Time: 6–7 hours   **Information:** BLM Office
Elevation Time: 2,000 feet   Palm Springs
Difficulty: Strenuous   (619) 251-4800

The Boo Hoff Trail takes the hiker deep into the Santa Rosa Mountains along the north drainage of Martinez Mountain, with wide, impressive vistas of the Salton Sea Basin. This interior trail leads into the wilderness areas where hikers find it difficult to believe that just over the hill is the sprawling Coachella Valley and the city of La Quinta. Along the way the trail treats you to a feeling of wild desert mountains and solitude and if you are lucky, some of the bighorn sheep living in the Santa Rosa Wilderness.

> **DIRECTIONS:** Follow the directions for the Lost Canyon Trail, until you reach the trail sign for the Boo Hoff Trail.

Continue up the Boo Hoff for the better part of 2 miles until the canyon drops down into the wash, just past the sprawl of cholla cactus. Continue up the trail, as it climbs up and out of the wash. You will continue to gradually climb 2 more miles. Along the way are numerous side canyons, dry falls and washes that are typical of the Santa Rosa Wilderness. Following a wet winter, sometime between mid-March and mid-April (but start early on the trail, as it gets hot this time of year) you will see rivers of flowers flowing from the canyon sides along the trail. These can be spectacular but must have enough water to really grow profusely.

At the western end of the Boo Hoff Trail, you will find yourself above La Quinta. From here you can turn around and head east, retracing the same route. Some hikers make a shuttle hike out of the Boo Hoff Trail by parking along the furthest back road in La Quinta (Calle Tecate) and following the wash/jeep road down to the street. By doing it this way, the hike one way is about 8–9 miles. The trail was affectionately named for Mr. Boo Hoff, a leading figure with the equestrian group The Desert Trail Riders.

*Family of barrel cactus
on the Boo Hoff Trail*

8 LOST CANYON via the BOO HOFF TRAIL

Length: 10 miles
Hiking Time: 5 hours
Elevation Gain: 1,500 feet
Difficulty: Strenuous

Season: October to April
Information: BLM Office
Palm Springs
(619) 251-4800

Of the many canyon hikes found in the foothills of the Santa Rosa Mountains, the Lost Canyon hike offers some of the most diversified terrain and breathtaking views. For the entire hike the massive, imposing form of Martinez Mountain looms above the hiker's southern view. During a rainy winter, the north face of the mountain is streaked with many rivulet-type waterfalls. These serve to accent the canyons emerging from the mountainside and feed the vegetation trapped in washes. Although plant life is sparse, cholla and barrel cactus along with ocotillo are abundantly dispersed throughout the length of the hike.

DIRECTIONS: Lost Canyon is reached by driving several miles east past the city of La Quinta on Hwy 111 and turning right onto Jefferson Street, proceeding until you reach the PGA West Golf Club. Turn left at PGA West (Avenue 54), right at the next stop sign (Madison) and right again at Avenue 58, following the signs to Lake Cahuilla County Park. Near the lake the road dips down after a rise and splits to the left and right. If you do not have a 4WD vehicle, park in the land area formed between the road split. If you can drive further, continue to the left until you approach the guard gate to the Quarry Golf Club, take a sharp left into the desert and onto a recognizable jeep road. Follow this east for several hundred yards, then south along the low foothills until you are stopped by the dike. Park here. Hikers must walk this road if they parked where the road splits.

Climb over the dike and onto the combination wash/jeep trail. It stays between 20 to 30 yards wide for the next .75 mile. During this time you are hiking a beautifully vegetated wash that offers views of the southern end of the Santa Rosa Mountains and the Salton Sea Basin to the southeast. As the trail narrows, bear to the right. You can see that you are coming up to a rather large canyon against the mountains. Look to the right for a black metal sign marking the beginning of the Boo Hoff Trail. Take this trail into the high foothills. You are truly away from it all at this point, as the wilderness canyons of the Santa Rosa Mountains impress the hiker with dry and sometimes wet waterfalls along the north face of Martinez Mountain.

As you ascend, look south. You will be following a large canyon which at this point in the hike begins to draw closer. After 1.5 miles on the Boo Hoff Trail you will begin to drop down into a thickly vegetated wash, after passing through an extensive stand of cholla cactus. Although the trail continues on the hillside past the wash, turn left into the wash and begin traveling down canyon. Stay to the right as you climb down several dry waterfalls until you come to the spectacular canyon drop that spills into Lost Canyon. Most hikers can negotiate this 150 foot drop without a rope. Stay to the left as you crawl down the rock falls and onto the trail above it. Continue bearing left and descend down into the canyon. Be especially careful of loose gravel and rock. This section looks awesome with it's view of the Salton Sea framed by the slopes of Lost Canyon, and might appear impassable. But children, with careful adults there to help, have done this section without incident, so it's as safe as the hiker is.

Take the canyon left for .5 mile until you reach another large dry falls. The trail can be found 15 to 20 yards before you reach the falls, and up on the hillside to your right. You will drop down into your final canyon. To the right, 200 yards, is a waterfall, generously flowing after a good rainfall. After seeing this last waterfall, turn back and continue down canyon for .5 mile until you see the Boo Hoff Trail marker to your left. From here it's a simple matter of following the wash back to your vehicle.

The Lost Canyon hike is impressive to desert dwellers for its cactus, soaring canyons, impressive views and most of all that unforgettable descent down the large dry falls that upon first glance leaves some hikers with a feeling of "no way!"

Lunch above Devil's Canyon

9 BEAR CREEK CANYON RIDGE

Length: 8 miles   **Season:** October to April
Hiking Time: 5 hours   **Information:** BLM Office
Elevation Gain: 2,000 feet   Palm Springs
Difficulty: Strenuous   (619) 251-4800

This hike is one of the many canyon hikes found along the foothills of the Santa Rosa Mountains. These mountains form the southern boundary of the Coachella Valley with Martinez Mountain dominating the southeast portion of this range. Bear Creek Canyon flows as a major drainage north from Martinez Mountain, towards the sleepy city of La Quinta. The ridge affords expansive views of not only the city, but in a single sweep of the eyes one sees both the Salton Sea and the distant, often snow capped San Jacinto and San Gorgonio peaks.

DIRECTIONS: To reach the trailhead take Hwy 111 to La Quinta and turn right (south) at Washington Street into La Quinta. Continue to Eisenhower Drive, turn right and follow Eisenhower until it ends at the back of town at Bermudas. Turn right, noting that Bermudas becomes Calle Tecate. Park where Tecate meets Madero. Looking to the south you will see broad, sandy flatlands bordered by low foothills to the right.

Begin walking south on the jeep trail that bears to the right towards the foothills until you reach a wall of boulders blocking the dirt road that drops into a wide wash.

Once in the wash, turn south (left) and favor the left for about a 20 minute walk. Chuparosa, with it's colorful red and orange blooms, is abundant, especially from February to April. As the canyon narrows, look for the small, sharply defined canyon to your right that shows charred rock from camper's use. Just past this canyon, at the Palo Verde tree, is the beginning of Bear Creek Ridge Trail.

For the first .5 mile stay on the established trail, being careful of false side trails which are often blocked by rocks. As you climb back into the massive canyon network you can feel a wild, distant land, void of any human influence. After 1.5 miles you begin to rapidly ascend the ridge, surrounded by ocotillo that dominates the landscape. Looking down to your left is the massive rocky canyon of Bear Creek, offering a good water flow during bountiful, wet winters.

After 2 miles plus, hikers will find themselves on a plateau from where they can see the mountain ranges surrounding the Coachella Valley, and the Salton Sea to the east. A lacework of canyons flowing from the Santa Rosas surround the trail in all directions. As you continue up the trail, the views to the north allow you to peek into Joshua Tree National Park. Still further up, the hiker is treated to hidden valleys deep in the interior mountains and culminating in a massive verdant oasis tucked into the fold of a canyon. Here you are over 4 miles from the trailhead. You can choose to lunch there or continue exploring to see what lies over the next ridge. There are no trails beyond the oasis, but any wash will lead you into either dry or flowing waterfalls, depending on how wet the winter has been.

La Quinta from Bear Creek Canyon Ridge

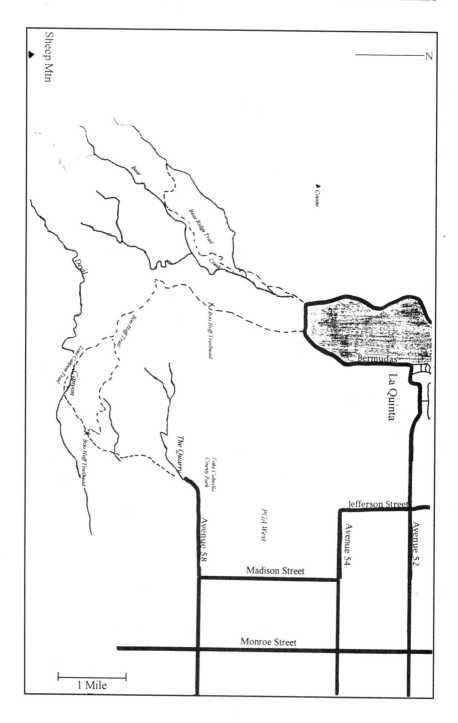

10 EISENHOWER PEAK LOOP

Length: 6 miles
Hiking Time: 4 hours
Elevation Gain: 700 feet
Difficulty: Moderate

Season: October to April
Information: The Living Desert
Palm Desert
(619) 346-5694

The Living Desert is a visitor's mecca for those wishing to learn more about the flora and fauna of the Coachella Valley. This Preserve has grown to include its own wildlife zoo. You will find walking paths that highlight varieties of plant and animal life found in the local desert. As you would expect, there is also a major hiking trail within the grounds that takes you up towards Eisenhower Mountain, whose 1,952 foot elevation corresponds perfectly to his election year! The trail is a good representation of desert terrain and makes a perfect beginning to your Living Desert tour.

DIRECTIONS: To reach the trailhead, turn south onto Portola Avenue from Hwy 111 in Palm Desert. After 2 miles you will see the entrance to the Living Desert on your left. From the main entrance turn right and follow the sidewalk and signs to the wilderness loop. Many docents are available to help direct you. Pick up a plant and tree guide as you leave the main building, as the plant life is well-marked along the trail.

After walking .75 mile to the end of the inner loop, then .75 mile to the Quail Guzzler, the canyon leg starts. This is very rugged terrain, marked by wash-walking and boulder-hopping. At the .75 mile marker post you begin to climb a very defined trail heading first east then north to the picnic tables. Eisenhower Mountain is directly on the right but you must bushwhack to the top, as there is no defined trail. The view from the top gives you a fabulous look at the whole of the Coachella Valley. After leaving the tables and heading down the ridge leg, you are treated to stunning glimpses of the estate homes of Eldorado and Vintage Country Clubs. Signs along the way highlight the history of both the palm trees and the trail itself. This section is an easy 1.5 mile meander back to the patio, book store, and a well deserved snack at the main buildings. In warmer months be sure to bring 2 quarts of a cool drink to quench the desert thirst.

Bighorn Sheep at Living Desert
Photo by Sue Bobek

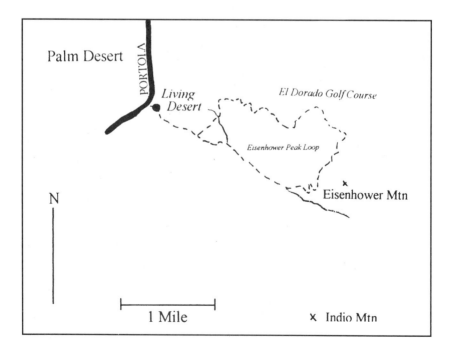

11 CARRIZO CANYON

Length: 4–6 miles
Hiking Time: 3–4 hours
Elevation Gain: 500 feet
Difficulty: Moderate

Season: October to April
Information: BLM Office
Palm Springs
(619) 251-4800

This is another Santa Rosa Mountain canyon hike that exposes the hiker to that special type of hiking known as canyon hiking. Most of this hike takes place in the canyon and is highlighted by a series of dry or wet waterfalls, depending on the amount of rainfall. In a wet season the hiker is treated to lush vegetation that hardly suggests the presence of the surrounding harsh desert, minutes from the narrow confines of the canyon interior.

DIRECTIONS: To get to Carrizo Canyon turn south from Hwy 111 in Palm Desert onto Hwy 74. After about 4 miles the highway begins to turn up the mountains just past the Bighorn Development to your right. You can park along the right shoulder about .25 mile after passing the large Santa Rosa Wilderness Area sign.

Drop down into the wash, or south of where you park, and hike up the wash as it veers to the left and on into Carrizo Canyon. It can be pleasantly cool here, even in the warmer spring months, but it is always wise to carry at least 2 quarts of a cool drink, no matter how cool the canyon is.

Continue along the canyon floor until you reach the first large falls and climb above it by scrambling up the right side. Be careful of wet rock or algae, and make sure your footholds are secure. You can continue up this canyon's many falls but be aware that this can be tiring. This is a great short hike

Barrel Cactus. Photo by Sue Bobek

that gives the hiker a sense of adventure, being on the edge enough to keep your attention, while showing the rocky inner of a typical desert canyon. As the trail continues up the side of the mountain it becomes more of a rock scramble and should be attempted only by hikers comfortable with this kind of combination hiking/scrambling.

12 ART SMITH TRAIL

Length: 16 miles
Hiking Time: 8 hours
Elevation Gain: 1,200 feet
Difficulty: Strenuous

Season: October to April
Information: BLM Office
Palm Springs
(619) 251-4800

This hike is a real treat for the hiker who enjoys a full day's journey without excessive elevation gains. The Art Smith Trail serves as a major link between the Palm Desert portion of the Santa Rosa Mountains and Palm Canyon's network of trails, including the Murray Peak area south of Cathedral City. This day hike allows you to penetrate the mountains while resting along the way in the several palm oasis that accent the trail.

> **DIRECTIONS:** To reach the trailhead, turn south from Hwy 111 in Palm Desert onto Hwy 74. After 4 miles you can park at the new Santa Rosa Mountains Visitor's Center on the left or on the right shoulder, away from the traffic, and adjacent to a water agency protective dike.

Climb the dike and drop down into a flat wash. Continue on the trail heading south towards the mountains and left of the nearby foothills and fence. After .25 mile you drop down into another wash. Turn right for .25 mile until you reach the first canyon to the right. Hike into the canyon, along the wash, and in 100 yards you will see the trail to the left that within a few hundred yards takes you to a large metal sign indicating "Art Smith Trail." This trail is named in honor of Art Smith, trail boss for many years with the Desert Riders.

The trail winds steeply up the mountain for .5 mile until leveling out. From here you can see the Bighorn Development below. The trail takes you through several palm oasis for the next 2 miles. During March/April, this section of the trail is abundant with plant life, barrel cactus and other colorful wildflowers and cactus in bloom . . . a real contrast with the stark look in autumn.

By the third mile you are hiking beneath the flat topped Haystack Mountain facing due south. As you continue, the cities of the valley floor look up from the north, but at times the trail takes you into sheltered areas where no civilization is apparent. After almost 5 miles, the trail crosses the upper reaches of Magnesia Canyon, a palm filled canyon that makes a sheltered lunch stop. Feel free to explore down canyon before continuing to the western end of the trail at Dunn Road.

Junction of Art Smith Trail with Schey Trail

Art Smith trailhead
Photo by
Sue Bobek

13 THE SCHEY TRAIL

Length: 6 miles   **Season:** October to April
Hikint Time: 3 hours   **Information:** BLM Office
Elvation Gain: 1,000 feet   Palm Springs
Difficulty: Moderate   (619) 251-4800

At the southern edge of Palm Desert, the Santa Rosa Mountains begin to dominate the landscape and provide a quick escape from the hustle of the thriving desert resort sprawling to the north. The Schey Trail is one of the first and quickest routes into these mountains and allows hikers a taste of the great outdoors and wilderness while being just minutes from downtown Palm Desert.

DIRECTIONS: To reach the trail, drive south from Hwy 111 onto Hwy 74. Turn west (right) on Cahuilla Way, the last street to the right before the Bighorn Development. Turn right again onto Cat Canyon Road, left on Cholla Way and right onto Paisano Road. Proceed north, half-way down Paisano Road and notice the wash to the left. Park and enter the wash, heading west, following the power lines.

After 1 mile the wash narrows and shortly you see on the left side a white arrow and sign indicating "Footpath to Art Smith 3 miles" painted on the rock.

The trail climbs into the foothills of the Santa Rosas, along switchbacks that generally proceed up most of the way. You will crest at about 1,500

Going down Schey Trail from Bighorn Overlook

feet where you will have an excellent view of the Bighorn Development beneath you. After 2 miles, a rock on the left says "Bighorn Overlook." Views are again noteworthy. Further up the trail you pass through a valley full of gorgeous boulders, then through a small wash, and finally at the 3 mile mark you join with the Art Smith Trail.

If you want a longer hike, just turn right on the Art Smith and go as far as you feel up to . . . 12 miles to Cathedral City! Less than a mile from the junction with the Art Smith Trail is a series of palm oasis with great views of the higher Santa Rosa Mountains. This trail can get very hot in the afternoon of early fall and late spring, so come with enough water. The views back down the trail show the outstretched Coachella Valley reaching beyond Palm Desert.

Desert Agave in early spring

14   MAGNESIA FALLS CANYON

Length: 6 miles
Hiking Time: 4 hours
Elevation Gain: 400 feet
Difficulty: Strenuous

Season: October to April
Information: BLM Office
Palm Springs
(619) 251-4800

The Coachella Valley is blessed with a variety of canyons found where the desert reaches into the surrounding mountains. Magnesia Canyon is a particularly stunning canyon to hike because of the many dry (and sometimes wet) waterfalls found within the canyon. These falls are higher than most found in the desert and require careful rock scrambling to safely negotiate them. This hike is classified as difficult for this reason, and should not be hiked alone. Some hikers find a 50 to 75 foot rope useful, but not necessary.

DIRECTIONS: To reach the canyon, drive Hwy 111 from Palm Springs to Rancho Mirage. Just past Bob Hope Drive turn right onto Magnesia Falls Drive and park at the very end of the street.

Begin hiking on the dirt road that heads west on top of the dike. As you approach the mountains, veer to the left and hike into the large canyon. You are now in Magnesia Falls Canyon.

There is no formal trail, but instead a wash that makes up the canyon floor. Within .5 mile of entering the canyon you will reach the first imposing falls, a sheer rock face thrusting upwards at about a 40 degree angle. Careful climbers can make their way up the slope and into the higher reaches of the canyon. Continue climbing the dry falls as you encounter them. Most hikers turn back after several miles of bushwhacking through this often overgrown canyon, having enjoyed the adventure of scrambling up the many dry falls. Experienced hikers can continue the full 6 mile length of the canyon, taking the left fork when the canyon splits and climbing above and right of the large falls. After 4 miles you will eventually intersect the Art Smith Trail. By turning left they can hike another 6 miles back to the Art Smith Trailhead. Shuttle vehicles placed at either end of the Art Smith and Magnesia Falls Canyon Trailheads make this hike a long 12 mile all-day adventure. We recommend hiking this longer version with someone who has done it before.

The first of many falls along the Magnesia Falls Canyon Trail Photo by Sue Bobek

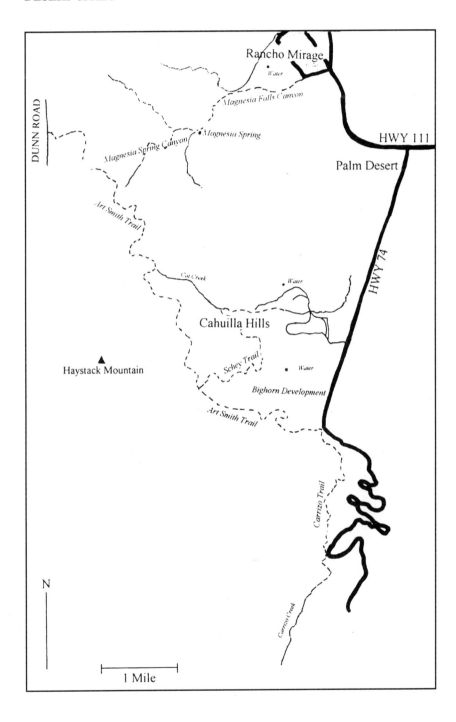

Rancho Mirage

Water

Magnesia Falls Canyon

DUNN ROAD

HWY 111

Magnesia Spring Canyon ● Magnesia Spring

Palm Desert

Art Smith Trail

HWY 74

Cat Creek

● Water

Cahuilla Hills

▲ Haystack Mountain

Schey Trail

● Water

Bighorn Development

Art Smith Trail

Carrizo Trail

N

Carrizo Creek

1 Mile

PALM SPRINGS AND INDIAN CANYONS

15 THE HAHN-BUENA VISTA TRAIL

Length: 16 miles
Hiking Time: 8 hours
Elevation Gain: 2,000 feet
Difficulty: Strenuous

Season: October to May
Information: BLM Office
Palm Springs
(619) 251-4800

The Hahn-Buena Vista Trail was named after Jean Hahn, a member of the Desert Riders and a very ardent equestrian. Buena Vista translates into "good view," and the 360 degree vistas afforded by this trail validates this choice of names. The trail itself is an isolated segment of the much larger network of trails surrounding the Murray Hill area east of Palm Canyon, and on the western most reaches of the Santa Rosa Mountains.

DIRECTIONS: To reach this beautiful section of trail, follow the directions to Fern Canyon, to where the Wildhorse Trail joins the secondary wash.

From here go left to the sign post for the Vandeventer/Hahn-Buena Vista Trail, turn right and follow the trail as it meanders through small washes and up short slopes to a Y intersection. Go left here, making what appears to be a northwest jaunt to Dunn Road.

At Dunn Road turn right (south) and continue to where the Art Smith Trail joins it. You will find some much appreciated picnic tables where you can rest. Turn right off the Dunn Road and begin following the Hahn-Buena Vista Trail back to the Wildhorse Trail and your eventual starting point. The views here are spectacular, and in a wet spring, wildflowers and blooming cactus accent the area.

This section of trail, as well as all the Murray Hill trail network, tends to warm up quite a bit on most fall or spring afternoons, so come prepared with adequate water and food.

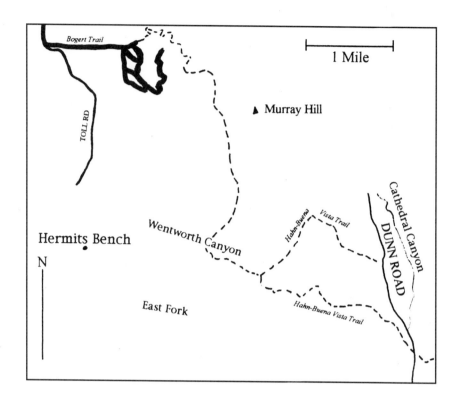

 16 **MURRAY HILL (PEAK)**

Length: 10 miles   **Season:** October to April
Hiking Time: 5 hours   **Information:** BLM Office
Elevation Gain: 2,100 feet   Palm Springs
Difficulty: Strenuous   (619) 251-4800

It's difficult to call Murray Hill anything but a "peak," yet officially it's a
hill on all the maps . . . unofficially after climbing the 2,100 feet to the
top, you'll think of it more like a PEAK! The views are magnificent, showing the region around Palm Springs, Cathedral City and Palm Canyon,
while offering you the nearby San Jacinto Mountains to the west.

DIRECTIONS: To reach the trail, drive on Hwy 111 in the east section of Palm Springs and turn south on Elk Trail. Park behind the 1905 Elks Lodge and hike up 200 feet in the steep, rocky canyon, staying to the left side of the canyon.

At the top there is a pile of concrete pieces; head left towards the wrecked yellow bulldozer. Follow the trail up the old road to the trailhead at the top.

Continue along the old jeep road in an easterly direction, making a partial circle around a small hill. Look southeast to see the looming singular massif of Murray Hill. Very shortly up the road and to the left is a rock cairn. Follow the trail down into Eagle Canyon. In spring this area can be a sea of yellow from the abundant brittle bush and other desert flowers. Continue to a Y intersection. Left is the Eagle Canyon palm oasis; continue following the Eagle Canyon Trail up and to the right for .5 mile until reaching the Eagle Canyon/ Palm Canyon/McManis trail signs. Follow the trail down to the wash at the bottom of Eagle Canyon and out the other side (north or left). The trail follows a bit of a ridge until you see the Clara Burgess trailhead sign. Take this trail up the remaining 2 miles to the top of Murray Hill.

Picnic tables await you at the top, and a stunning 360 degree view of the surrounding deserts, Dunn Road to the south, and the stately San Jacinto Mountains due west. To return, you can retrace your route or continue south on the Clara Burgess Trail, down the south side of Murray Hill to the trail sign. From here hike in a westerly direction along a beautiful ridge with stunning vistas. At the bottom of the switchbacks, turn right at the huge trail sign, walking in a northerly direction until rejoining Eagle Canyon Trail. From here return the way you came.

Eagle Canyon Trail leading to Murray Hill

17 FERN CANYON

Length: 10 miles
Hiking Time: 5 hours
Elevation Gain: 1,200 feet
Difficulty: Strenuous

Season: October to April
Information: BLM Office
Palm Springs
(619) 251-4800

Fern Canyon offers the hiker the surprise find of a generous outgrowth of ferns growing in a cactus-filled desert! The hike allows you great views of the South Palm Canyon near Hermit's Bench (the Indian trading post) and good vistas of Palm Springs and the nearby San Jacinto Mountains and canyons.

DIRECTIONS: This hike begins by taking Hwy 111 into Palm Springs and then turning onto South Palm Canyon to Bogert Trail, heading east over Palm Canyon Wash. Turn left on Barona Road. The trailhead begins east of the road barricade.

Follow the trail up along a barbed wire fence, 50 yards to the trail signs "1966 DV Garstin & Earl Henderson." Proceed right, up the Garstin Trail and many switchbacks for 2 miles to the next sign post marking the Wildhorse/Berns/Shannon/Garstin/Palm Canyon trails. Go right at this sign post, continuing on the Garstin Trail. Shortly you come to a Y . . . keep right. Continue for another mile to the trailhead sign for Fern Canyon/Vandeventer/Hahn-Buena Vista/Art Smith/Palm Canyon. Continue up, walking the ridge while viewing Cathedral City (north) and South Palm Canyon (south). Hike .75 mile until reaching a Y intersection and Clara Burgess Trailhead. Stay right (south) onto a plateau/wash. In spring this area is alive with blossoms from cactus, encelia, scrub brush . . . a carpet of color!

Follow the gentle sloping wash down to where

Palm Canyon as seen from the Indian Trading Post

a second wash joins from the north (left). Proceed right towards **Palm Canyon.** Eventually you are rewarded with a lush palm oasis, where a huge boulder is located, covered with dripping water and gorgeous ferns. From here you can either backtrack or continue into **Palm Canyon** and the Indian trading post if water levels permit.

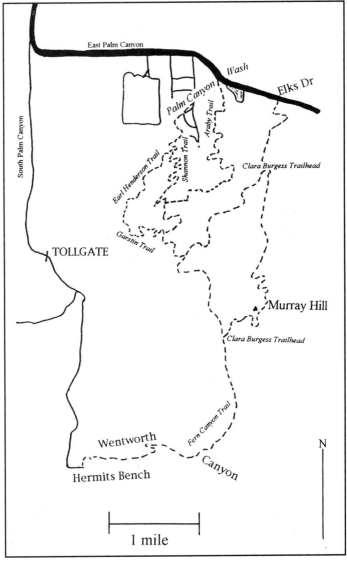

Murray Hill/Fern Canyon/Earl Henderson Trail/Shannon Trail Loop/The Araby Trail

18 PALM CANYON TRAIL to LITTLE PARADISE

Length: 8 miles
Hiking Time: 5 hours
Elevation Gain: 1,000 feet
Difficulty: Moderate

Season: October to April
Information: BLM Office
Palm Springs
(619) 251-4800

Hikers often refer to the destination of this hike as "Little Paradise" for good reason. This trail takes you through the lush jungle-like river bottom of Palm Canyon, out onto back country high desert plateaus from where the entire horizon opens up. The trail looks 14 miles south towards the distant Santa Rosa Mountains, while impressing you with the surrounding, soaring San Jacintos thrusting up from the canyon floor, stunning views of the desert and Palm Springs to your rear and finally . . . to a series of magnificent plunging cliffs, waterfalls, exotic pools fed by crystal clear, shimmering ribbons of water racing through slot-like rock gorges. What are we waiting for . . . let's go!

> **DIRECTIONS:** Begin this hike by reaching Palm Canyon in the Agua Caliente Indian Canyons south of Palm Springs, as described in the Palm Canyon Trail hike.

As you pass the right fork of Palm Canyon, veer left and follow the stream bed and trail for another .5 mile until reaching the marker indicating that the trail crosses the stream and climbs up the south bank and the ridge above. Head south along this trail. Very soon the climb takes you out into the open country where the full, magnificent beauty of these canyons can be appreciated. The trail stays on a high plateau, with some occasional looks into small adjacent canyons. After 2 miles of hiking you reach a wide dirt wash-jeep road. Take the trail straight ahead, rather than following the wash to the left. You eventually arrive at a place where the trail melts away into the sandy rock, but is still faintly visible on the slowly climbing rise above the canyon to your right. For this reason it is best to travel here with someone knowledgeable of these parts i.e., the Coachella Valley Hiking Club and its members/trail guides.

The trail drops down into a gully and demands you scramble up the far slope . . . slippery with loose gravel so caution is advised. Once at the

Pools at Little Paradise

top, favor the faint trail as it climbs to the left and begins taking you above the canyon. As you climb, walk to the west ridge and gather in the stunning views of the canyon below. You continue to follow the trail above the canyon and finally come to a high drop off looking down into a massive rocky gorge, accented by a plunging waterfall shooting through a narrow rock slot. The trail takes you past the gorge (you can walk down into this gorge and explore to your heart's content but be careful of the smooth rocks) and after .5 mile, down alongside a tranquil rock-enclosed series of pools, a favorite lunch spot, where you can explore further down canyon in and above the river.

After lunch, climb out to the east and rejoin the trail for a wild hike above a series of rock gorges and waterfalls. Continue to take extra care, as the rock is loose and the sand, slippery. After another .5 mile, the trail drops almost into the stream. Here you can exit this trail by bushwhacking to the southeast for a distance of less than 100 yards where you will join the main Palm Canyon Trail, found here as an almost road-like pathway.

Take the Palm Canyon Trail north . . . it eventually follows a wash and connects to where you first crossed this same wash earlier in the day. Look for the rock ducks on the upper slope indicating the way back. The Indian Canyons close at 5PM, so watch the time if you are planning a hike back through the stream bed before reaching this main section of the trail for the hike to the trading post.

Waterfalls at Little Paradise

19 PALM CANYON TRAIL to BULLSEYE ROCK

Length: 8 miles   **Season:** September to April
Hiking Time: 5 hours   **Information:** BLM Office
Elevation Gain: 700 feet   Palm Springs
Difficulty: Moderate   (619) 251-4800

For centuries, the Agua Caliente Indians inhabited the magnificent canyon lands south of Palm Springs and Palm Canyon. You would expect to find some artifacts and signs of human habitation somewhere in or near Palm Canyon, and on this hike you do. The main draw, however, continues to be the stunning and expansive scenery, as Palm Canyon is ringed by dozens of adjacent canyons, while looking up to the high country mountains of Desert Divide and San Jacinto Mountain. The destination of this hike is a large, rounded, granite slab thrusting up from the canyon floor known as Bullseye Rock. A stream flows beneath its towering mass and encourages the lush, jungle-like growth found in this section of upper Palm Canyon. A fire in 1994 severely burned this area, so vegetation is only now making a comeback.

DIRECTIONS: To reach the trail, follow any hike direction given in this guide for Palm Canyon Trail.

Once on the trail, continue on the southeast canyon fork (the main Palm Canyon Trail) until reaching the sign directing you up the southern hillside and into the backcountry (see the Palm Canyon to Little Paradise hike).

This trail is best done with someone who has been to Bullseye Rock before, as some bushwhacking is required. Follow the Palm Canyon Trail for almost 1.5 miles after climbing out of the main palm-filled canyon. You will eventually come to a steep gully on your right marked with rock ducks. Follow this gully down the 20 to 30 yards to the small stream, then cross over, keeping a close watch for the trail on the other side. This trail takes you up a hill and onto a plateau known as Indian Potrero. It was here in a small village that the Agua Caliente Indians once resided. All that remains are several grinding stones 12 to 16 inches deep, formed in some of the surrounding rocks. The trail climbs higher into the backcountry until reaching a small stream drainage and follows this rivulet to Bullseye Rock, the obvious round granite mass to your left. You can ascend this rock without a rope, but a 75 foot length will assist you around the more sheer challenges. Lunch at the top for a great view of the canyon country around you or continue exploring on the trail . . . but note that cactus infestation is thick in these parts and the trail is sometimes difficult to follow.

Granite monolith of Bullseye Rock

20 PALM CANYON TRAIL to the RIGHT FORK

Length: 4 miles
Hiking Time: 4 hours
Elevation Gain: 400 feet
Difficulty: Strenuous

Season: September to June
Information: Indian Canyons
Tollgate
Agua Caliente
Indians
Palm Springs

This is a "wild canyon scramble" through twisted rock formations, along and sometimes in a rushing stream, with lush groves of massive Washingtonia palms providing a jungle like setting. Palm Canyon is the jewel of the many canyon hikes found in the sprawling Agua Caliente Indian Canyons south of Palm Springs. It is not as easy a hike as it looks. The rocks are very slippery, and the current can be surprisingly strong during peak snowmelt and runoff. Families can do this hike only by staying above the stream, and only adventurous hikers who are used to negotiating rock obstacles and scrambling through water hazards should continue into the right fork canyon as described here.

DIRECTIONS: To reach the trailhead, drive through Palm Springs on Hwy 111 until reaching the juncture with South Palm Canyon Drive. Turn onto South Palm Canyon and proceed 2 miles to the Indian Canyons tollgate, then continue 2.5 miles to Palm Canyon and the trading post. The trail begins down the walkway from the trading post and to the right.

For the first .75 mile you are treated to a pathway above the stream, contorted rock formations forming the river bed with assorted pools (and often sunbathers) at various intervals and a stunning concentration of palm trees accented by vines, cottonwoods and desert plants made so by the abundant water supply.

As the trail reaches back into the canyon you eventually come to the first major canyon fork on the right. This is where only serious hikers (mountain goats) should tread. You can follow the right fork for miles . . . but the first 2 miles will provide challenge enough. There are deep pools to hike through or around, tricky cliff formations, huge boulder scrambling and plenty of swimming holes to try. Caution . . . until sometime in March the water is COLD snow melt. After that, water levels subside, water temperatures rise and the trip gets a whole lot easier! Be prepared to encounter small groups of gutsy day hikers, college kids and isolated sun worshipers . . . this canyon is no secret!

Right Fork of Palm Canyon

The right fork of Palm Canyon makes the perfect "adventure" hike for those prepared to deal with the challenges and a great picnic getaway for those inclined to laze on a warm spring day on the rocks beside shimmering canyon pools.

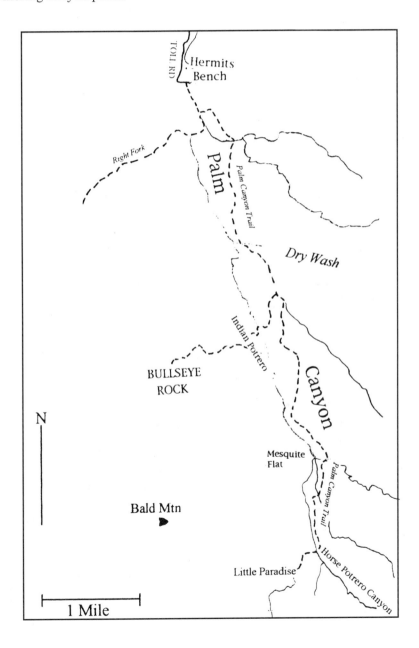

21 MURRAY CANYON TRAIL

Length: 6 miles
Hiking Time: 4 hours
Elevation Gain: 500 feet
Difficulty: Moderate

Season: September to June
Information: Indian Canyons
Tollgate
Agua Caliente
Indians
Palm Springs

Murray Canyon Trail takes you deeper into the lower reaches of the San Jacinto Mountains via a palm enclosed canyon stream found on the Agua Caliente Indian Reservation in south Palm Springs. This canyon differs somewhat from its close neighbor, San Andreas Canyon, by offering the hiker many more miles of trail on which to explore higher canyon elevations. The California fan palm is also quite abundant in Murray, giving another lush escape from the surrounding desert heat. This hike requires more caution during high spring runoff, as the stream bed tends to challenge the trail at several crossings. You can also travel further up Murray Canyon in bushwhacking style, depending on your own adventuresome spirit, the thickness of the undergrowth, and strength of the rushing waters.

> **DIRECTIONS:** Reach this trail by following directions for the San Andreas Canyon, found at the south end of Palm Springs in the Agua Caliente Indian Canyons, 2 miles south of Hwy 111 on South Palm Canyon Drive.

When you reach San Andreas Canyon, cross the stream and follow the signs south of the river. The trail meanders awhile through the underbrush and along the stream before beginning to break away from its sister canyon and head in a more southwest direction. Desert willow, assorted cactus and a scattering of cottonwood are found along the river. Take extra care along this waterway during strong and high runoff . . . hikers have been injured on the slippery rocks or in the deep water. This hike makes a great picnic adventure and treats you to the vistas of high canyon country and soaring cliffs.

*San Andreas
Canyon with
Desert Divide
Ridge above*

22 THE WEST FORK TRAIL to SAN ANDREAS CANYON

Length: 10 miles
Hiking Time: 6 hours
Elevation Gain: 2,500 feet
Difficulty: Strenuous

Season: October to April
Information: BLM Office
Palm Springs
(619) 251-4800

The West Fork/Jo Pond Trail climbs dramatically and steeply upwards out of Palm Canyon, eventually reaching the Pacific Crest Trail and Desert Divide, 6,000 feet above the valley floor. After 2 miles, the trail joins with another section heading north and climbing to reach a maximum elevation gain of 2,500 feet. By taking this right fork the hiker can make his/her way back to San Andreas Canyon, thereby requiring a shuttle car to be parked there and at the Indian trading post in Palm Canyon. You are treated to the most magnificent vistas of the high country above Palm Springs, as well as the long palm-filled canyons below.

DIRECTIONS: To begin, reach the Palm Springs Indian Canyons south of town and described in the Palm Canyon hikes.

Just after several hundred yards down the Palm Canyon Trail, look to the right for a sign post marking the beginning of the West Fork Trail.

You climb through a wonderland of rocks and mountain vegetation, noting as you ascend how radically fast the scenery opens up below you. This trail is steep and strenuous. It can be demanding in warm weather. Hikers should bring plenty of water and be careful of overextending themselves on a hot day.

The trail brings you to a lovely picnic table alongside a rushing stream and surrounded by lush greenery. This could be the halfway point for hikers not wishing to do the total 10 miles or who have not made provisions for a shuttle.

From here the trail picks up across the stream and begins another rapid ascent up the mountain. The views continue to amaze. During late winter the slopes are ablaze with flowers and by spring the cactus follow suit. You continue on this trail until it begins to emerge overlooking Murray Canyon to the north. The trail then descends down to the lower slopes and crosses several streams, notably Murray Canyon . . . you might find the crossing difficult in wet winters but continue downstream until you do connect with a good crossing point. The trail picks up on the other side and eventually joins with the Murray Canyon Trail, taking you back to the parking lot in San Andreas Canyon.

West Fork Trail climbing out of Palm Canyon

Petroglyph found on the West Fork Trail
Photo by Sue Bobek

23 MAYNARD MINE TRAIL

Length: 10 miles   **Season:** October to April
Hiking Time: 6 hours   **Information:** BLM Office
Elevation Gain: 2,200 feet   Palm Springs
Difficulty: Strenuous   (619) 251-4800

Alongside the mountainous ridge rising above Murray Canyon on the
western side of Agua Caliente Indian Canyons is a rugged trail leading
up to the remains of an old tungsten mine, worked during World War II,
and known as the Maynard Mine, after its developer, Jim Maynard. This
hike not only takes you to the scattered remains of the mine, but gives
the hiker great views of the canyon slopes across Palm Canyon Valley as
well as the snowy ridge line of Desert Divide. This is a great winter hike,
taking you closer to the Pacific Crest Trail above the valley, while showing you the swirling clouds and storms associated with the upper ridge.

Begin on the Murray Canyon Trail as it makes its way quickly up the mountain. In short order you will come to a rock marker indicating a trail rising from the Murray Canyon Trail, and heading in a steep fashion up another ridge. This is the Maynard Mine Trail.

The climb up the slope is relentless . . . nothing gradual about it. No shade covering is offered so hikers doing this trail in October or a warm March must be prepared for warm weather hiking. You essentially hike on rocky slopes so that the heat is reflected back by the rocks. After 5 miles you reach your objective, the Maynard Mine.

All that remains is a 10 foot deep hole which you can examine, and an old gas-powered engine, rather large, suggesting the strenuous work it took to haul it up the same slope you just hiked. Return by the same trail, treated to the many beautiful vistas of the valley and the distant peaks to the south.

Maynard Mine Trail

24 SAN ANDREAS CANYON

Length: 2 miles
Hiking Time: 2 hours
Elevation Gain: 50 feet
Difficulty: Easy

Season: September to June
Information: Indian Canyons
Tollgate
Agua Caliente
Indians
Palm Springs

Tucked away in the southwestern corner of Palm Springs is a hiker's paradise situated on several thousand acres of the Agua Caliente Indian Reservation, locally known as "the Indian Canyons." The canyons there join with the foothills of the soaring San Jacinto Mountains rising from the canyon floor and culminating in the 10,801 foot San Jacinto Peak. The Pacific Crest Trail (PCT) looks down into these canyons from the south by southwest mountain ridge, Desert Divide, bordering the reservation, while during the winter, torrents of water wash through the canyons below. Many spectacular hikes begin or end in these canyons. One of the shorter, but still quite lovely hikes is the San Andreas Canyon hike, found less than a mile from the tollgate. This trail follows a stream (sometimes river during peak mountain runoff) while winding through hundreds of native California fan palms. The towering snow-capped mountains above suggest to the hiker that countless hiking adventures await at higher elevations.

DIRECTIONS: To reach San Andreas Canyon, drive south onto South Palm Canyon Drive where it meets Hwy 111 in the south end of Palm Springs. Follow the signs to the Indian Canyons, and after paying the toll, take the road to the right .75 mile to the picnic tables.

The trail follows the right side of the stream while crossing over several times before bringing you to a wire fence exactly 1 mile from the start. This stream can be quite high after heavy rainfall or when the snows melt in the mountains above the desert, usually in late February. The lush palms, vines, bushes and cactus along the stream suggest a more tropical setting and contrast sharply with the desert below. Be careful of slippery rocks and hard-to-negotiate places. San Andreas makes a great picnic or romantic get-away hike . . . but even the kids find high adventure as they make their way under towering cliffs and through the rushing stream. March, early April and late October are especially fine times to hike this and other canyons found in the Indian Canyons.

Cliffs above San Andreas Canyon

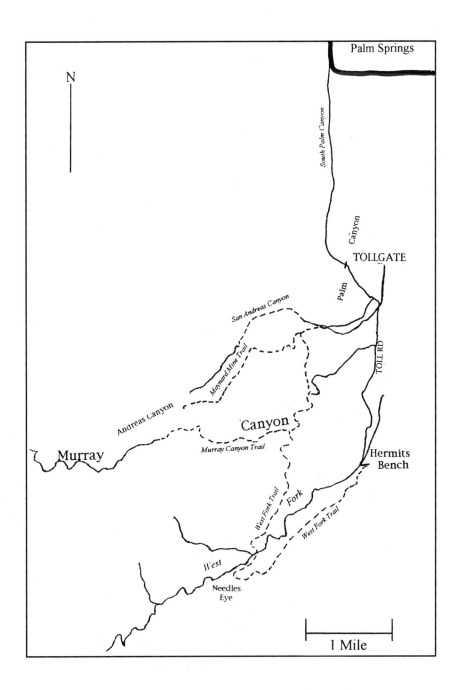

1 Mile

25 EARL HENDERSON TRAIL

Length: 4 miles   **Season:** October to May
Hiking Time: 3 hours   **Information:** BLM Office
Elevation Gain: 400 feet   Palm Springs
Difficulty: Easy   (619) 251-4800

This trail is one of the many interconnecting trails found on the ridges and plateaus surrounding Murray Hill, east of Palm Canyon. This trail is named after Earl Henderson, past president of the equestrian group, the Desert Riders. At the top of this trail, you are rewarded with scenic views of Canyon Country Club, South Palm Springs and the San Jacinto Mountains thrusting up from the west side of Palm Canyon.

DIRECTIONS: From Palm Desert, go west to Palm Springs via Hwy 111 and Palm Canyon. Turn left (south) onto Araby Drive, proceed through Palm Canyon Wash and park on the left-hand side of the road.

Head west up the wash for about .25 mile to the Palm Springs Trail sign. Turn left and follow the trail up to the Henderson and Shannon Trail signs. Continue southwest on the Earl Henderson Trail. After 2 miles, the trail ends at the Garstin Trail sign. From here, you are treated to a vista view of South Palm Springs, Palm Canyon and Canyon Country Club. This makes a great early morning or evening hike, short, but with just enough elevation gain and good views to make the effort worthwhile.

Canyon Country Club beneath Earl Henderson and Shannon Trails

# 26 SHANNON TRAIL LOOP

Length: 7 miles   **Season:** October to May
Hiking Time: 4 hours   **Information:** BLM Office
Elevation Gain: 1,000 feet   Palm Springs
Difficulty: Moderate   (619) 251-4800

The Shannon Trail Loop is one of several beautiful variations of hiking loops offered by the unique interconnections of crisscrossing trails found in and around Murray Hill, on the eastern side of Palm Canyon. This loop gives you good views of the Palm Springs area and the nearby San Jacinto Mountains. The trail was named after Shannon Corliss, daughter of the Desert Riders' past president, Ray Corliss.

DIRECTIONS: To reach the trailhead, drive east on Hwy 111 towards Palm Springs and turn south (left) onto Araby Drive. Proceed through Palm Canyon Wash and park on the left or south side of the wash.

Head west up the wash for .25 mile to the trailhead sign, Palm Springs Trail. Turn left and up the switchbacks until reaching the signs for the Earl Henderson and Shannon Trails. From here, view Canyon Country Club and Palm Springs.

To make the loop, continue along the Earl Henderson Trail until reaching the sign post for the Garstin Trail. Follow the Garstin Trail up to the overlooks of South Palm Canyon and the sign post for Wildhorse/Bern/ Shannon/Garstin and Palm Canyon. Continue straight ahead in a northerly direction for a short distance to the next sign post, Garstin/Shannon/Henderson. From here, proceed left down the trail, quite steep in places, and take the Shannon/Henderson Trail back down to your starting point. This trail loop makes a wonderful early morning hike in spring, but take care to avoid hot desert afternoons, and always bring a good supply of water.

27 THE ARABY TRAIL

Length: 6 miles   **Season:** October to May
Hiking Time: 3 hours   **Information:** BLM Office
Elevation Gain: 800 feet   Palm Springs
Difficulty: Moderate   (619) 251-4800

The Araby Trail could also be dubbed the "trail to the stars," as it climbs above the Bob Hope Estate and the home of the late Steve McQueen. The view of these magnificent homes is readily available on this trail, along with that of Palm Springs, below. The Araby Trail is another great short but sweet "exercise" trail, allowing you to make the up and back trip in under 6 miles.

DIRECTIONS: From Palm Desert, drive west to Palm Springs on Hwy 111. Turn left (south) at the Rimcrest/Southridge Road and development. The trail can be found on the left (east) side of the road, shortly after turning.

As you hike up the Araby Trail, you are in for 3 miles of spectacular scenery and homes. The trail skirts the home of Bob Hope as it makes it's way to the top of the ridge, before connecting with the Berns/Garstin/ Henderson Trail. At the sign post for these trails one can return to the trailhead or continue and eventually interconnect with the many other trails found in these foothills. Bring plenty of cool water if you do this hike in late spring or early fall. Afternoon temperatures can approach 100 degrees.

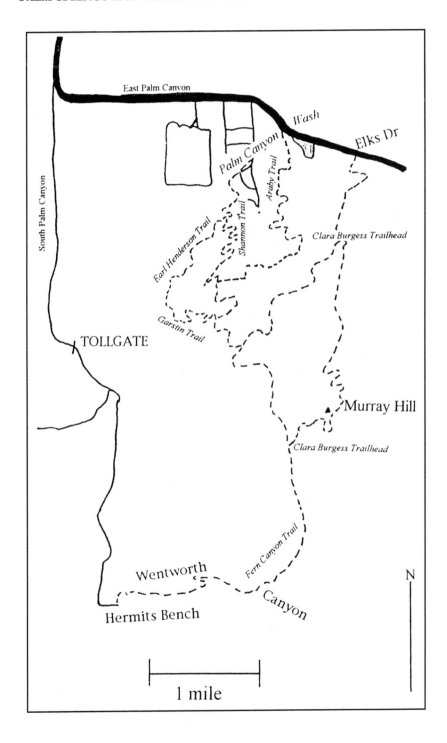

East Palm Canyon

Wash

Elks Dr

Palm Canyon

South Palm Canyon

Araby Trail

Earl Henderson Trail

Shannon Trail

Clara Burgess Trailhead

Garstin Trail

TOLLGATE

Murray Hill

Clara Burgess Trailhead

Fern Canyon Trail

Wentworth

Canyon

Hermits Bench

N

1 mile

28 NORTH and SOUTH LYKKEN TRAIL

Length: 9 miles   **Season:** October to March
Hiking Time: 5 hours   **Information:** BLM Office
Elevation Gain: 800 feet   Palm Springs
Difficulty: Moderate   (619) 251-4800

In 1972 the Skyline Trail was renamed the Lykken Trail in honor of Carl Lykken, a Palm Springs pioneer and the town's first postmaster. This magnificent desert view trail travels along the San Jacinto Mountains above Palm Springs, roughly following Palm Canyon Drive. The views of Palm Springs and the valley stretching towards the eastern horizon are awesome as you negotiate through the rocky terrain, accented in the spring with the yellow blooming brittle bush and flowering cactus. En route to the end of South Lykken Trail you are treated to fabulous views of Palm Springs and Tahquitz Canyon, held sacred by the Cahuilla Indians and abounding in vegetation and waterfalls but restricted in use due to environmental abuse.

DIRECTIONS: To begin hiking the South Lykken Trail, drive into Palm Springs via Hwy 111 which becomes Palm Canyon, and turn south onto South Palm Canyon. Proceed south to Canyon Heights Road; 250 feet further along on the west side of the road is a trail sign. This is a shuttle hike. Cars need to be parked here. The shuttle spot for the Lykken Trail is Cielo Drive off Panorama Road in Palm Springs.

Head west up the trail; before the switchbacks begin, you will come to the trailhead sign. The trail continues for 3 miles before it goes down to street level at Tahquitz Creek. Go north through Tahquitz Creek following the trail signs (if there has been heavy rainfall or snowmelt, go over the creek by using the cement water dike). Meander over and down La Mirada Street until it meets Ramon. This marks the beginning of the North Lykken Trail.

The trail switchbacks as it heads northwesterly towards Chino Canyon. After several miles you reach the picnic tables overlooking the Palm Springs Desert Museum. Continue to take the trail north, as if heading around the corner of the mountain. The trail meanders down through a wash full of large rocks and desert growth. On the other side of the wash you have a gradual climb towards Chino Canyon, where the trail ends in a subdivision by descending the faint trail on the north side of the picnic table.

There is no shade on this trail so bring plenty of cool water.

29 THE PALM SPRINGS DESERT MUSEUM TRAIL

Length: 2 miles
Hiking Time: 2 hours
Elevation Gain: 1,000 feet
Difficulty: Moderate

Season: October to May
Information: Palm Springs
Desert Museum
(619) 325-0189

The Palm Springs Desert Museum is a cultural landmark in Palm Springs for all valley residents and visitors . . . an oasis of both natural history and desert flora and fauna and the finest in art and cultural entertainment. So what better way to immediately involve yourself in the desert hiking scene than by walking out of the Desert Museum and onto the challenging Museum Trail found just outside their front door? The view from the top gives you a great look into the sprawling city of Palm Springs and the desert beyond. While a steep hike of over 1,000 feet in just a mile, if you take it slow and steady, most hikers can reach the picnic tables found at the trail's end with little trouble.

DIRECTIONS: To reach the trailhead, drive into Palm Springs on Hwy 111 until reaching the downtown area. Turn west on Tahquitz Way, then right on Museum Drive. The museum is found directly in back of the Desert Fashion Plaza Mall. The trail begins in the north parking lot of the museum.

After steeply ascending the mountain, it connects with the Carl Lykken Trail.

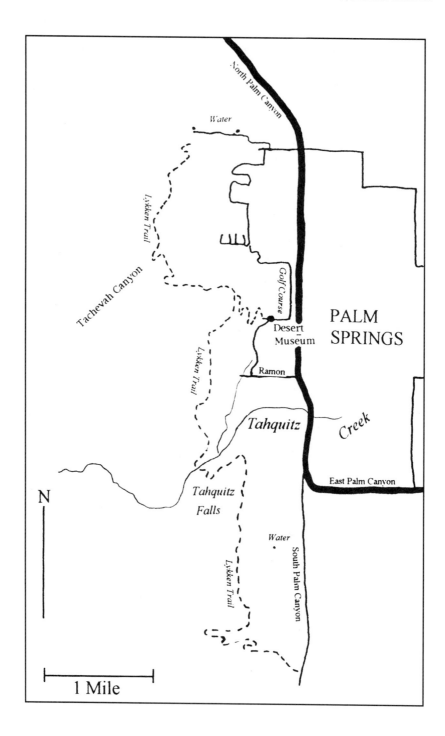

North Palm Canyon

Water

Lykken Trail

Tachevah Canyon

Lykken Trail

Golf Course

Desert
Museum

PALM
SPRINGS

Ramon

Tahquitz   *Creek*

East Palm Canyon

Tahquitz
Falls

Water

South Palm Canyon

Lykken Trail

N

1 Mile

SAN JACINTO MOUNTAINS

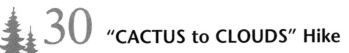

30 "CACTUS to CLOUDS" Hike

Length: 22 miles
Hiking Time: 13 hours
Elevation Gain: 10,400 feet
Difficulty: Very Strenuous

Season: May and October
Information: BLM Office
Palm Springs
(619) 251-4800

Crossed the Sahara Desert lately? Swam the Amazon River recently? Did a Boston Marathon last week? Have we got a challenge for you! In all of the continental United States there is perhaps no higher elevation gain in one day than the "Cactus to Clouds" . . . hike? From the beginning of the trailhead, this hike takes you up, and up, and up . . . 10,400 feet to the top of San Jacinto Peak . . . all in one day, all 22 miles of it!

The views of the Coachella Valley and surrounding mountain ranges are spectacular. The views of the seemingly impossible top are, too! But be in the best shape of your life to handle this one. One consolation . . . you get to ride the tram down to Palm Springs, instead of descending those 10,400 feet!

DIRECTIONS: Drive into Palm Springs on Ramon Road from I-10 and park at the road's end.

Take the Lykken Trail, up the switchbacks, for about 1.5 miles until reaching a coffee table size boulder on the left side of the trail. Painted on this boulder is a sign, "Long Valley 8 miles" (Long Valley is the valley adjacent to the mountain tram station at 8,600 feet elevation).

This section of the trail looks down into Tachevan Canyon to the right (north) for about 2.5 miles. Although this early section of the trail is some-what easy to find, the remainder of the trail to the top of Long Valley is faint, poorly marked and should be done only with someone who has previously hiked this section. This entire trail is virtually an unending succession of upward reaching switchbacks—perhaps a respectable "hiking cousin" to the famed 97 switchbacks to Mt. Whitney.

There is no water available on this trail until you reach Long Valley. Up to the Ranger Station in Long Valley is almost 11 miles (about 8 hours hard hiking). From this point exhausted hikers may opt to make the short walk to the tram station and catch the next tram down to Palm Springs (don't feel too bad, many who have attempted the "Cactus to Clouds" saga have done just that).

If continuing, you will need a wilderness permit from the Ranger Station. The trail from here is clearly marked and well used. From the Ranger Station proceed to Round Valley, then up to Wellman Divide. Here, the last section of trail takes you almost directly to San Jacinto Peak. One third mile from the peak is the side trail that will take you to your final destination. Several hundred yards from the peak is a stone cabin which serves as a necessary shelter in poor weather conditions.

Once on the peak, you enjoy a 360 degree view—of what seems like the whole world.

Down valley view from "Cactus to Clouds" Trail
Photo by Sue Bobek

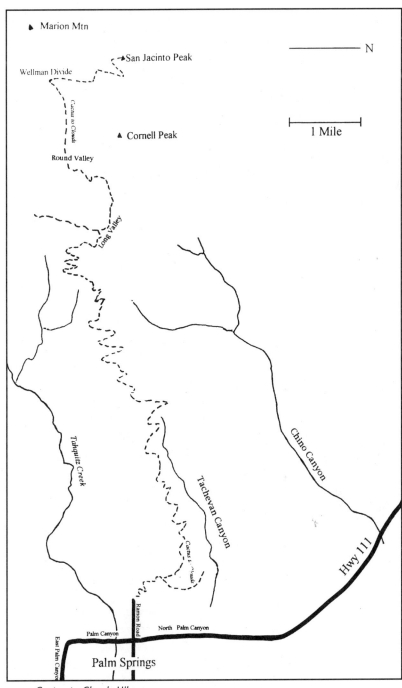

Cactus to Clouds Hike

31 PALM SPRINGS AERIAL TRAMWAY to SAN JACINTO PEAK

Length: 11 miles   **Season:** May to November
Hiking Time: 6 hours   **Information:** USDA Forest
Elevation Gain: 2,300 feet   Service, Idyllwild
Difficulty: Strenuous   (909) 659-2117

John Muir, the famous naturalist, exclaimed after climbing to the top of San Jacinto Peak that the view from San Jacinto was one of the most sublime spectacles seen anywhere on earth. This kind of endorsement is enough to get any serious hiker up the slope to the top! The peaks in the San Jacinto Mountain area are huge granite massifs that remind the well-traveled hiker of the High Sierras, especially the chain of peaks from Lone Pine to Bishop. The 360 degree view from the top gives you a complete reference for all of southern California's mountain and desert landmarks, and on a very clear day, you can actually peer into Nevada! The San Jacinto Mountains are relatively young—geologically speaking . . . perhaps 20 million years young. But the rocks in these mountains have been upthrust from deep within the earth and are perhaps 500 million years old! The hike to the top is varied, with the lower elevations offering sylvan meadows and streams before bringing you into the more demanding final climb up the Alpine slopes near the peak.

DIRECTIONS: To begin this adventure, take Hwy 111 exit into Palm Springs from I-10, or Hwy 111 from Palm Desert to Palm Springs. From the Interstate exit, drive 9 miles to Tramway Road then turn right and drive until reaching the parking area. Shuttle trams will take you to the Tram Station on crowded days. After paying the fee, ride the tram to the top, exit out of the Mountain Station and head towards the ranger station located .25 mile to the west. Obtain your day hiking permit, sign in, and take the trail leading to Round Valley.

During the early summer you cross many streams or travel alongside them, but by early fall most have dried up. The trail winds up through the pine thickets until coming to beautiful Round Valley. Here the grass is deep green, tall and richly watered . . . look for deer munching tender plants.

Continue towards the peak by taking the trail to Wellman Divide. This is a short, steep climb that begins giving you premonitions of views to come as you look back to the north and east into the desert below. At Wellman's Divide the views are spectacular, both of the Tahquitz Peak area and further Santa Rosa Mountains. From this point you are only 2.7 miles from the peak. Follow the trail to the top, up steep switchbacks. The views continue to amaze, as vistas grow ever more expansive and breathtaking. Near the top there is another trail junction: take the one for San Jacinto Mountain. In a short time you come to and then pass a stone shelter for those caught in stormy weather. Just up from there is the peak.

Geographers claim that the angle of descent, the steepness of San Jacinto Mountain from top to base, is the sheerest in the United States. From the top looking down, most tend to agree. It can be quite cool at the top, even cold and very windy. Bring a windbreaker, a pair of binoculars . . . and enjoy the view!

San Jacinto Mountain

32 PALM SPRINGS AERIAL TRAMWAY to SADDLE JUNCTION LOOP

Length: 12 miles
Hiking Time: 7 hours
Elevation Gain: 3,000 feet
Difficulty: Strenuous

Season: May to November
Information: USDA Forest
    Service, Idyllwild
    (909) 659-2117

The top of San Jacinto Mountain and Wilderness Area is shaped in the form of a bowl, whose west side is considerably higher than the eastern. This geographical feature allows hikers to do a magnificent loop hike from the Mountain Tram Station towards Saddle Junction above Idyllwild. The route follows a gradual descent from the high point of the "bowl" at Wellman Divide down to the bottom at Saddle Junction, along the bottom of the valley floor, and then finally up to the northern top ridges near the starting point. Hikers are treated to wide vistas that reinforce the notion of San Jacinto Mountain being an "island-in-the-sky," dominating the western boundary of the Coachella Valley.

> **DIRECTIONS:** To reach the trailhead, follow directions for the Tram to San Jacinto Mountain hike. Take Hwy 111 into Palm Springs, turn up Tramway Road and park. After riding up to the top of the mountain, head for the rangers station .25 mile west of the Mountain Station. Sign in and pick up your wilderness permit for your day hike to Saddle Junction.

Follow the trail up to Wellman Divide. This first 3 mile leg takes you 1,200 feet through pine forests, along mountain streams that are quite full in early summer and alongside the lush green grasslands of Round Valley. At Wellman's Divide you first glimpse the expansive horizon vistas that will fill your vision for the better part of the next 2.5 miles. The towering granite massif of Tahquitz Peak dominates your view to the southeast.

As you head down the trail you pass a series of small but delightful springs flowing from the mountainside and encouraging a proliferation of ferns, flowers and grasses. Descending further, you pass the junction with the Pacific Crest Trail (PCT), then head rapidly down to the pine groves surrounding Saddle Junction. You usually find a number of hikers gathered there, as this is the main crossroads for the hikes above Idyllwild.

Continue back to the Tram by taking the trail from Saddle Junction north and west of Skunk Cabbage Meadows. This section of trail is populated by huge Ponderosa pines, some say the largest in California. You will soon come to the cool waters of Willow Creek. Take a good rest here; for the next 2 miles the trail winds steadily up the mountain, but offers you good views of the Desert Divide and Santa Rosa Mountains to the southeast.

You finally reach the top of the "bowl" and can soon see the Tram Station in the near distance. Bring at least 3 quarts of water, as this hike begins cool but can end warm.

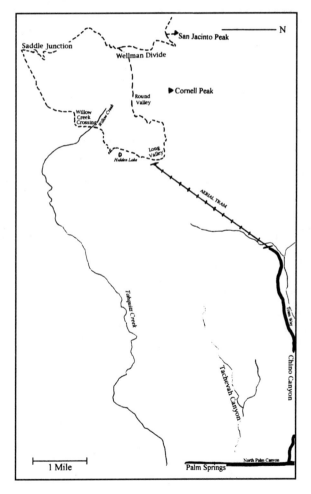

33 JO POND TRAIL to CEDAR SPRING

Length: 7 miles   **Season:** Year Around
Hiking Time: 4 hours   **Information:** USDA Forest
Elevation Gain: 1,700 feet   Service, Idyllwild
Difficulty: Moderate   (909) 659-2117

In 1994 the Jo Pond Trail connecting Palm Canyon in Palm Springs to the south terminus at the Cedar Spring Trailhead was completed. This magnificent 13 mile trail allows hikes to either climb to the PCT in the San Jacinto Mountains at Desert Divide and drop down into Palm Canyon along the West Fork Trail or reverse direction. Hikers need to arrange a car shuttle at either end, have someone drop them off and pick them up when finished or have two groups hike in opposite directions and exchange car keys. The best times of the year are late October to late November and from mid-winter to April. The Jo Pond Trail treats the hiker to spectacular vistas of the Coachella Valley and surrounding mountains and, like its cousin the Pines-to-Palms Trail, gives a variety of desert and mountain flora to enjoy along the way.

DIRECTIONS: To reach the south terminus trailhead for the Cedar Spring section, take Hwy 74 south from Palm Desert off Hwy 111, 28 miles to Morris Ranch Road in Garner Valley. Turn right at the fire station and continue 3.5 miles to where the road ends and a sign indicates to park off pavement.

Park here and follow the road, on foot, for 100 yards until you see the sign for the Cedar Spring Trail. Within minutes you are walking along a delightful stream in a grove of beautiful oak, provided you hike from January to April. You will soon see the large sign indicating the Jo Pond Trail with mileage to various highlights along the way. The trail continues through a meadow, green and well flowered, from April to May, then climbs for 1.5 miles up a series of switchbacks until reaching the top of the PCT at Desert Divide. This first 3 mile section can be very hot during the late spring through summer. Hikers need to assess if a Pacific offshore breeze is blowing. During these times it can be 110 degrees in the desert below, but 65 degrees on this section of the trail. Also watch for ticks.

The hiker has several options when they reach the top of the crest. I suggest you first take the right fork to the east and explore for a mile or so, then return to the crest and continue down the desert side for 1 mile until reaching Cedar Spring. This is a beautiful lunch spot or rest area. Many hikers choose to camp here before exploring nearby trails. You will find a generous number of incense cedar and black oak, with running water nearby. The return trip views the Palomar Mountains to the south.

Meadows along the Cedar Spring Trail

34 JO POND TRAIL to FOBES SADDLE OVERLOOK

Length: 9 miles
Hiking Time: 5 hours
Elevation Gain: 1,200 feet
Difficulty: Moderate

Season: Year Around
Information: USDA Forest
Service, Idyllwild
(909) 659-2117

The Pacific Crest Trail (PCT) that follows the ridge line of the San Jacinto Mountains takes the hiker through many scenic sections that yield spectacular views of the Santa Rosa Mountains to the southeast and the San Jacinto Mountains as they run northwest and culminate at San Jacinto Peak. Always drawing the hiker's attention along this section is the Coachella Valley that sprawls beneath the mountains and ends at the Salton Sea Basin. This grand vista hike, the PCT along the San Jacinto

Range, also offers the hiker an opportunity to see terrain that suggests someplace other than the more harsh desert conditions below. Valley residents can quickly escape their sandy wasteland by accessing the PCT at the Jo Pond Trailhead's south terminus and enjoy an invigorating hike through pine forests found by hiking west where the Jo Pond Trail intersects the Desert Divide. This section eventually takes you to an expansive overlook that shows the entire eastern flank of San Jacinto Mountain.

DIRECTIONS: To reach the trailhead, follow the directions for the Jo Pond Trail to Cedar Spring.

Once you begin the hike it is 2.5 miles to the Desert Divide ridge and the PCT. Here, turn left up the mountain. As you climb, look often to the rear and take in the views of the many mountain ranges, the Santa Rosas as well as Martinez Mountain, due east. This section makes a marvelous "snow hike" from January to March. The snow is sometimes only 4 to 6 inches deep but you will still come away feeling like you've experienced real winter conditions.

You crest the mountain after only .5 mile. Beneath you is the long thin trail of Palm Canyon coming out of Palm Springs to the north and ending in the Santa Rosa Mountains to the south. As you continue west you will be amazed by the spectacular peak system of the San Jacintos, a feature that fills the entire western skyline. This view is made more beautiful if the winter snows have been generous. Hikers taking this trail in late October and early November are treated to fall colors made by the thick stands of oak found along the ridge.

After 1.5 miles along the ridge, you come to a sign that indicates "trail" going down into a thick pine forest. Before taking this trail, walk another 25 yards to the rocky point south of this sign. This makes a great lunch spot with magnificent views of the eastern flank of the San Jacinto Mountains. Continue through the pine forest and eventually you reach Fobes Saddle Overlook showing you the low saddle along the ridge trail as you look down and west. The return hike treats you to more spectacular mountain vistas, as your vision encompasses the Santa Rosa Mountains filling the eastern horizon.

35 JO POND/CEDAR SPRING TRAIL to PALM CANYON TRADING POST

Length: 13 miles   **Season:** October to April
Hiking Time: 8 hours   **Information:** BLM Office
Elevation Gain: 1,300 feet   Palm Springs
Elevation Loss: 5,850 feet   (619) 251-4800
Difficulty: Strenuous

For sheer, majestic vistas and spectacular spring flora, few trails in or near the Coachella Valley match up to the Jo Pond/Cedar Spring Trail, done the entire length from atop the Desert Divide Ridge/Pacific Crest Trail (PCT) to the Indian Trading Post in Palm Springs. This is a shuttle hike. Someone must drop you off at the Cedar Spring Trailhead in Garner Valley and pick you up at the Indian Trading Post in Palm Canyon. The best time for this adventurous hike, both regarding temperature and flora/river runoff, is March to mid-April. The views are inspiring and beautiful, as you hike up and over the Desert Divide Ridge, make your way along West Fork Canyon and finally emerge over the sprawl of Palm Canyon before reaching the Trading Post at the canyon's head. Take your camera, hope that the snow is still blanketing the higher peaks, and be prepared for the rigors of an almost 6,000 foot drop in elevation . . . protect those knees and toes!

> **DIRECTIONS:** To reach the trailhead, drive 28 miles south on Hwy 74 from Palm Desert and Hwy 111, or almost 11 miles east of Mountain Center on Hwy 74 if you come in from Hemet. Turn north onto Morris Ranch Road at the CDF Fire Station, and proceed 3 miles to the sign that says "Park Off Pavement." After parking, pick up the trail for Cedar Spring just a few hundred yards up the road.

You spend the first .5 mile walking through beautiful oak woods, along a rushing stream and over a stunning meadow before beginning the ascent up the slope to the PCT and Desert Divide Ridge. At the trail's beginning, a large sign marking the southern terminus of the newly built Jo Pond Trail indicates 3 miles to Cedar Spring, 7 to the picnic tables above West Fork Canyon, and 12.5 to the Indian Trading Post (it says 15 miles to the Tollgate which is 2.5 miles beyond the Trading Post).

As you climb towards the PCT, looking south you see the Palomar Mountain Observatory atop Palomar Mountain and sections of Garner Valley. Once at the crest, and beginning your descent over the ridge, the entire Coachella Valley spreads out before you, with Palm Canyon's 16 mile length snaking it's way far beneath you to the east. After a mile you reach the cool, incense cedar grove and camping area of Cedar Spring. From here the trail should be signed, indicating a climb from the campground, along a stream/gully and eventually over to the burnt mountainous area northwest of Cedar Spring, made that way from the July '94 fire.

Once over this section, you are hiking along the Garnet Ridge for 3 to 4 miles, with awesome high country views to the west of the entire length of the San Jacinto Mountains, made especially scenic with a thick winter snow cover. Palm Canyon continues to amaze you as you look east, with noticeable green patches, tree-filled canyons and the obvious meandering trail along its bottom.

After 7 miles of the trail steeply dropping down the ridge, with dozens of switchbacks, you reach the beautiful picnic area and overlook, complete with several picnic tables . . . a great and natural lunch stop. From here the scenery really captures your esthetic sense, as the trail comes down along the West Fork Canyon and offers you green valleys, waterfalls, grass covered slopes, oases, stunning verdant canyons, flowers and flowering cactus. This part of the hike is more like a trip through a nature preserve than through "desert canyons"!

After almost 12 miles, you finally come over the ridge looking into verdant Palm Canyon. The trail quickly takes you to the canyon's bottom along a short section of raging stream and up to the Indian Trading Post for a richly deserved cool drink. This hike does test your ability to come down a steep trail . . . strong knees are a must!

Jo Pond Trailhead

Trail's end—in the Palm Canyon

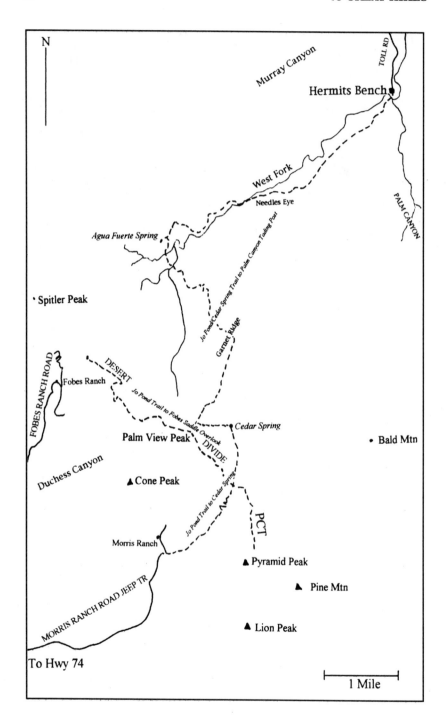

N

Murray Canyon

TOLL RD

Hermits Bench

West Fork

PALM CANYON

Needles Eye

Agua Fuerte Spring

Jo Pond/Cedar Spring Trail to Palm Canyon Trading Post

• Spitler Peak

Garnet Ridge

FOBES RANCH ROAD

DESERT

Fobes Ranch

Jo Pond Trail to Fobes Saddle Overlook

Cedar Spring

Palm View Peak

DIVIDE

• Bald Mtn

Duchess Canyon

▲ Cone Peak

Jo Pond Trail to Cedar Spring

PCT

Morris Ranch

▲ Pyramid Peak

▲ Pine Mtn

MORRIS RANCH ROAD JEEP TR

▲ Lion Peak

To Hwy 74

1 Mile

36 THE ERNIE MAXWELL SCENIC TRAIL

Length: 5 miles
Hiking Time: 3 hours
Elevation Gain: 300 feet
Difficulty: Easy

Season: May to November
Information: USDA Forest
Service, Idyllwild
(909) 659-2117

The Ernie Maxwell Scenic Trail is the perfect leisurely hike, especially for families. This trail is marked by gentle contours, an occasional stream, and a generous mix of Jeffrey, Ponderosa and Coulter pines, with some incense cedar and fir. The trail bears the name of the local Idyllwild resident, Ernie Maxwell, to honor his pioneering conservation efforts and his love of the surrounding mountains.

> **DIRECTIONS:** To hike this trail, follow the directions for reaching the Devil's Slide Trail at Humber Park, taking Fern Valley Road out of Idyllwild. Just before reaching the topmost parking area you will see the sign marking the entrance to the Ernie Maxwell Trail. No permit is needed for this trail.

Enjoy the gentle, quiet trail as it works its way through the forest thickets; September and October are especially nice months for walking this scenic route. The trail ends at a dirt road, where you simply return back to the trailhead.

37 HUMBER PARK—DEVIL'S SLIDE TRAIL to CARAMBA OVERLOOK

Length: 14 miles
Hiking Time: 8 hours
Elevation Gain: 3,400 feet
Difficulty: Strenuous

Season: June to November
Information: USDA Forest
Service, Idyllwild
(909) 659-2117

San Jacinto Mountain stands like a cool sentinel rising from the hot desert floor of the Coachella Valley. From late spring to early fall, hikers refresh themselves in the 8,000 foot forests above the valley floor, and by hiking one of the most spectacular desert overlooks at Caramba, gaze with relief into the searing deserts below. The view stretches all the way to the Salton Sea east, while encompassing the Santa Rosa Mountains to the south.

DIRECTIONS: To make this spectacular hike to the overlook, follow the trail directions for taking the Devil's Slide Trail at Humber Park out of Idyllwild. This hike requires a wilderness permit, which can be picked up at the ranger station in downtown Idyllwild.

After 2.5 miles you come to the Saddle Junction intersection. Head for Laws Junction through and past the lovely Tahquitz Creek Valley, with it's running streams and lush emerald grasses. After 4.7 miles you reach Laws Junction, which makes a perfect lunch spot, highlighted by the beautiful sylvan water setting of Willow Creek.

The trail to Caramba Overlook leaves from Laws Junction and is a 2 mile descent through thinning forests to the rock formations known as Caramba. If the winter has been wet, you can find good water in nearby Tahquitz Creek, and even a running waterfall found by scrambling down a ways from Caramba. This can be a very hot trail at the height of summer, so come prepared with ample water.

From Caramba, view the quiet desert below and the distant mountain ranges surrounding the Coachella Valley before starting the long climb back to Idyllwild.

38 DEVIL'S SLIDE TRAIL to SADDLE JUNCTION

Length: 5 miles
Hiking Time: 3 hours
Elevation Gain: 1,700 feet
Difficulty: Moderate

Season: May to November
Information: USDA Forest
Service, Idyllwild
(909) 659-2117

Devil's Slide Trail is the most frequently used access trail to the glorious hiking and sylvan beauty found in the San Jacinto Wilderness area and along the many miles of trail crisscrossing San Jacinto Mountain. From this trail, the hiker gets wonderful views of Marion Mountain, Suicide and Lily Rocks as well as great exercise in a short distance of 2.5 miles. By reaching Saddle Junction you are at the main focal point of several key trails heading off in all directions, including the Pacific Crest Trail (PCT). Because this is a very well-used trail, especially during summer, hikers are advised that day permits for the Devil's Slide are limited on weekends and holidays between Memorial Day and Labor Day and need to be picked up at the Forest Service Office in Idyllwild.

DIRECTIONS: To reach this trailhead drive into Idyllwild from Hwy 243 from Banning and I-10 or Hwy 74 and 243 from Palm Desert. In Idyllwild, take the Fern Valley Road to Humber Park (about 2 miles from downtown). Park as the road begins to turn around at the trailhead and loop back on itself. Be advised that on busy weekends you need to get there early.

The trail starts right up the mountain along a series of steep switchbacks. You can see Suicide Rock to your left and the huge granite monolith of Lily Rock to your right rear . . . both popular for serious rock climbers.

The trail crosses 6 or 7 small streams flowing down the mountainside, some of which flow all summer if the snowfall was heavy. The views are breathtaking as you look back down into Idyllwild and to the south. It may only be 2.5 miles to the top, but if you explore around Saddle Junction in the morning and descend late afternoon during the summer, it can be quite hot, so bring a good supply of water.

Lily Rock from Devil's Slide Trailhead

For years, Devil's Slide and the generous trail system found at the top, has offered a cool respite for the desert dwellers of the nearby Coachella Valley. The perfect ending for the perfect day is a well-deserved late lunch at one of the many fine restaurants in Idyllwild.

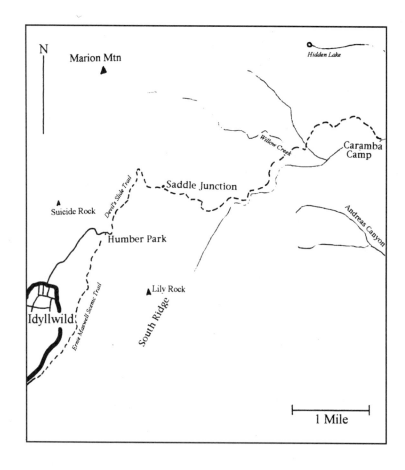

39 DEVIL'S SLIDE TRAIL to TAHQUITZ PEAK LOOKOUT LOOP

Length: 13 miles
Hiking Time: 7 hours
Elevation Gain: 2,500 feet
Difficulty: Strenuous

Season: May to November
Information: USDA Forest
    Service, Idyllwild
    (909) 659-2117

This loop hike gives the hiker a chance to see the full range of peaks and valley views from the southern portion of San Jacinto Mountain and Wilderness Area. It is a strenuous full day of exploring the ridges and vistas found above Idyllwild and can either be a shuttle from the Devil's Slide Trailhead to Tahquitz Peak Lookout and down to South Ridge Road where cars can be parked at both trailheads, or a full loop made by returning to Humber Park via the Ernie Maxwell Scenic Trail.

DIRECTIONS: To begin this demanding yet spectacular loop, follow the directions for reaching the Devil's Slide Trailhead. This hike requires a permit from the Forest Service Office in Idyllwild and a maximum 15 is allowed in any one party.

After reaching Saddle Junction, take the trail to the right for Tahquitz Peak. During the next mile plus, you gradually ascend along a ridge that affords you dramatic views of the desert to the north and the flanking eastern slopes of San Jacinto Mountain. You reach a crossroads of several trails after hiking 1.4 miles. From there take the trail to the south as it makes its way up to the Tahquitz Peak Lookout. This section of the hike is dominated by granite mountains and steep slopes, less forested than at the lower elevation. You reach the lookout tower, then head down the trail to South Ridge Trailhead. If you made this a full loop and not a shuttle, then once down South Ridge Road to where it meets Tahquitz View Drive, turn right up the road for about a mile until it meets the south end of the Ernie Maxwell Trail. This is the trail that will take you back to your vehicles at Humber Park.

40 DEVIL'S SLIDE TRAIL to LAWS JUNCTION

Length: 10 miles
Hiking Time: 5 hours
Elevation Gain: 2,000 feet
Difficulty: Strenuous

Season: May to November
Information: USDA Forest
    Service, Idyllwild
    (909) 659-2117

The lush green meadows and scented pine forests of Tahquitz Valley invite the hiker to escape the warm summer lowlands of Southern California and the blistering desert of the Coachella Valley surrounding the sky-island of San Jacinto Mountain. Once at the top, you are treated to soft green and celery colored grasses populated by a scattering of ferns and skunk cabbage, watered by the cool mountain streams of Tahquitz and Willow Creek.

> **DIRECTIONS:** To reach this sylvan paradise, follow the road directions to the Devil's Slide Trailhead at Humber Park in Idyllwild.

Take the Slide Trail to Saddle Junction. There, the trail divides into several routes. Take the middle route to Laws Junction. In about a mile you will reach the cool, green meadows of Tahquitz Valley and Tahquitz Creek. As you head north towards Laws Junction, you will see a grassy field to your right surrounding a small rocky outcropping. Make for the rocks and enjoy a quiet snack next to Tahquitz Creek . . . deer often are seen drinking at the water's edge.

Continue down trail through great stands of Ponderosa pine until you reach Laws Junction. Lunch alongside beautiful Willow Creek. This is a spot of rare beauty, cool, serene and a welcomed half-way spot during a warm a summer's day.

The route back is best made by following the trail left, avoiding the trail to Caramba Overlook. After a peaceful lunch you might find this section tiring, as it rapidly and unrelentingly climbs from the valley floor back to the trail heading south to Saddle Junction. You are rewarded, however, by several stream crossings and a picturesque look into the desert below. Be sure to bring adequate cool water, as these mountain trails can be very hot in summer. A day permit is required for this and every hike that begins with the Devil's Slide Trail.

Suicide Rock

41 DEVIL'S SLIDE TRAIL to RED TAHQUITZ OVERLOOK

Length: 11 miles
Hiking Time: 6 hours
Elevation Gain: 2,000 feet
Difficulty: Strenuous

Season: May to November
Information: USDA Forest
Service, Idyllwild
(909) 659-2117

This series of trails leads to an overlook near Red Tahquitz Mountain and gives the hiker great views of the Desert Divide Ridge, the Santa Rosa Mountains and Tahquitz Valley. The trail takes you into the backcountry, onto the Pacific Crest Trail (PCT), and finally down through the cool, green watershed of Tahquitz Valley and Tahquitz Creek. This day hike allows you to feel and experience the wide diversity of all the various mountain eco-systems found along the south and eastern flanks of the San Jacinto Mountain Wilderness.

DIRECTIONS: Begin this wonderful hike by following the Devil's Slide Trailhead directions given in previous hikes.

Make your way up to Saddle Junction, take the far right trail towards Tahquitz Peak for 1.4 miles until reaching the junction. Head down and east towards the trail for Red Tahquitz and Little Tahquitz Valley. The views here are wide and magnificent as you head into the valley. At the first junction turn right, up along the PCT. After one mile you come to a large fallen dead tree along the right side of the trail. Look up and to your right, and begin bushwhacking up the 50 feet of slope, down a small gully and up again until the high ground is reached. This is the lookout over the entire Desert Ridge Trail. You don't actually reach Red Tahquitz Peak, but this lunch spot offers stunning views to reward your scramble.

When returning, follow the trail down into Tahquitz Valley, then left where the sign indicates a return back to Saddle Junction. The lush green here offers a stark contrast to the rocky overlook near Red Tahquitz Peak.

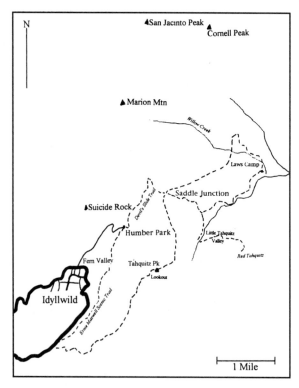

42 HURKEY CREEK TRAIL

Length: 3 miles
Hiking Time: 2 hours
Elevation Gain: 300 feet
Difficulty: Easy

Season: May to November
Information: Hurkey Creek
    Campground
    Hurkey Creek
    (909) 659-2050

South of the Desert Divide Ridge and the PCT in Apple Canyon, the mountains slope down and across a valley to reach over to Thomas Mountain. Hurkey Creek drains this area and a county-run campground can be accessed for reservations from April 1 to October 21. The area around Hurkey Creek is quiet, scenic and offers a convenient campsite for those coming from either the Coachella Valley or metropolitan Los Angeles. A short but very scenic trail winds its way out of the campground and into the surrounding higher elevations. For day hikers wanting an easy hike, this trail fits the bill. From May to early June, flowers are in bloom along its path and gentle vistas of the surrounding mountains complete the simplicity of the trail.

DIRECTIONS: To reach the trail and campground, drive on Hwy 74 out of Hemet, to almost 4 miles past the junction of Mountain Center and Hwy 243, or drive south on Hwy 74, 32 miles from Hwy 111 in Palm Desert. At Apple Canyon Road, across from Lake Hemet, turn north and then take a sharp left into the campground. The trail begins at the far west/southwest part of the campground.

In early spring, be prepared for water and runoff spilling across and alongside the trail. The hike follows a wide dirt trail, climbs onto a nearby plateau and, if the brush has been cleared, leads back into the campground. Most hikers prefer to walk to the scenic open spaces, admire the view and smell the flowers before turning back.

View towards Red Tahquitz from Hurkey Creek Trail

43 FOBES SADDLE to SPITLER PEAK and APACHE SPRING

Length: 6 miles
Hiking Time: 4 hours
Elevation Gain: 1,800 feet
Difficulty: Strenuous

Season: March to December
Information: USDA Forest
Service, Idyllwild
(909) 659-2117

The advantage of the Fobes Saddle Trail is the quick access it gives the hiker to the Pacific Crest Trail (PCT). This section of the PCT/Desert Divide is known for its ruggedness, chaparral and scrub brush and continues to take the hiker closer to the larger mountain mass of San Jacinto.

DIRECTIONS: To get to the trailhead, take Hwy 74 south from Palm Desert for almost 30 miles. After passing Morris Ranch Road, begin looking to the right for the large sign indicating Fobes Saddle Trail. The entry past the sign is through a metal gate left open during the day. This road to the Fobes Saddle Trailhead is not paved and is more safely done by 4WD vehicle. If the winter was particularly rainy, expect sizable potholes, washouts and rough conditions. For these reasons, this trail is not nearly as popular as the Cedar Spring PCT access at Morris Ranch.

The trail begins after a 3 mile drive down the dirt road. There is a very fast switchback of .75 mile up to the ridge and the PCT. Turn left and up the mountain through brush and forest thickets. If the trail has not been well maintained, you will find the going slow. The views of the Coachella Valley are beautiful but the vegetation is more wilderness scrub. Continue for almost 2 miles to Spitler Peak, rising above you to the south. After the peak, continue west until you see the sign for Apache Spring, a 500 foot descent down the mountain. If the winter snow has been heavy this section might have several feet of snow to contend with.

Fobes Saddle is the dip above the word 'Ranch' in the sign

44 THE ZEN CENTER to RED TAHQUITZ OVERLOOK

Length: 12 miles   **Season:** May to November
Hiking Time: 7 hours   **Information:** USDA Forest
Elevation Gain: 2,500 feet   Service, Idyllwild
Difficulty: Strenuous   (909) 659-2117

There are vista hikes all along the PCT ridge of the San Jacinto Mountains. However, this section of trail has many hikers' vote for being the most scenic and spectacular. It is one of the favorite hikes done by the Coachella Valley Hiking Club and offers a stunning variety of vistas and terrain. The trail is not on many maps because the first section of the trail begins on private property at the Zen Center east of Idyllwild. The Zen Master in residence allows hikers to use this trail but with several cautions. Bring as few vehicles as possible. Hike quietly for the first .5 mile, to avoid disturbing the meditation and tranquillity of those staying at the Center. Keep groups small and no dogs allowed.

DIRECTIONS: To reach the trailhead, drive 3.5 miles east of the Hwy 74/Mountain Center junction, or approximately 33 miles south of Palm Desert on Hwy 74. Turn onto Apple Canyon Road and continue almost 4 miles until reaching the large Retreat Center that looks like a hotel. Drive down the dirt road found to the right of where the paved road ends and next to a small fence, until you reach the Zen Center. Park in the small dirt area just before entering the grounds.

The trail begins north of the parking area and meanders through the Center's scattering of cottages and trailers. Ducks mark the trail. You continue this way for almost .5 mile until the trail appears to end in a grove of beautiful incense cedar, converging along a quiet stream. Look up and to the left to find the trail marked as it begins climbing the hillside through thickets of bush, pine, yucca, and manzanita. Keep a sharp eye for the trail, as it seems to sometimes merge into other side trails.

The ascent up the mountain is a steep 1,200 foot gain in just over a mile. Be careful of the cactus and slippery trail conditions. Once at the top, to the right, you will find a log resting place for a well-deserved break. The trail intersects the PCT a few feet north of the logs. Although the day's hike is to the west, take the trail to the right, east for .5 mile up and alongside the mountain. This section is highlighted by awesome sheer drops into steep rocky canyons and colorful rock formations. You finally turn a corner and see a 200 yard rock overlook to your left. Hike out to the end for the most awesome views of this entire desert and mountain region. Return to where the trail heads west from the log rest stop. You are treated along the way to splendid canyon views of West Fork and Murray Canyons, rising steeply out of Palm Canyon below you. The trail is an adventurous hike beneath the ridge of the mountain and some-times actually reaches the crest from where you can see towards San Diego and the Pacific Ocean. The views along this hike cannot be over-stated. They make you feel glad to be alive and glad you took up hiking! There is an exhilarating feeling of openness all during the hike. As you head ever closer to the view of Red Tahquitz and massive San Jacinto Mountain, you can look down the entire length of the Coachella Valley to the Salton Sea, accented by the equally exciting view of the mountain ranges extending to Anza Borrego Desert.

The hike ends when you come to a granite saddle from where Red Tahquitz Peak looks all so very close but is still many miles of strenuous hiking away. If you have the stamina you can continue to Red Tahquitz. The return hike gives you miles of great vistas all the way to where the trail begins down to the Zen Center. Here, be very careful. The trail is steep and the footing is slippery. Remember to observe silence or at least quiet conversation as you approach the Zen Center.

Red Tahquitz in the center

45 SPITLER PEAK TRAIL

Length: 10 miles
Hiking Time: 6 hours
Elevation Gain: 2,000 feet
Difficulty: Strenuous

Season: Year Around
Information: USDA Forest
  Service, Idyllwild
  (909) 659-2117

This trail to Spitler Peak is the most direct route up the mountain that allows the hiker to avoid lengthy sections of the Pacific Crest Trail (PCT) in attempting to reach the peak. The views at the top show the panorama of the Santa Rosa and San Jacinto Mountains with glimpses of the Palomar Range to the south.

DIRECTIONS: Reach the trailhead by following the directions for the Zen Center hike. Turn up Apple Canyon Road 3.5 miles south of the Hwy 74 and Mountain Center junction (Hwy 243) or about 33 miles south of Palm Desert on Hwy 74. At nearly 3 miles you will see the sign for the Spitler Peak Trail on the right road shoulder. Park here and begin the climb to the peak.

The trail winds steeply up through manzanita and other chaparral brush. If the trail has been properly maintained, as it usually is, the ascent up the slope is relatively unimpeded. Once at the top, you can choose to head either east towards Fobes Saddle and down to the trailhead or west to where the PCT meets the Zen Center Trail. Either way, you must arrange a shuttle. Each of these hikes is close to eight miles long and are described in previous hikes. The trail to Spitler Peak is a short .5 miles from where the PCT meets the trail coming up from the trailhead.

Desert Divide Ridge from Garner Valley

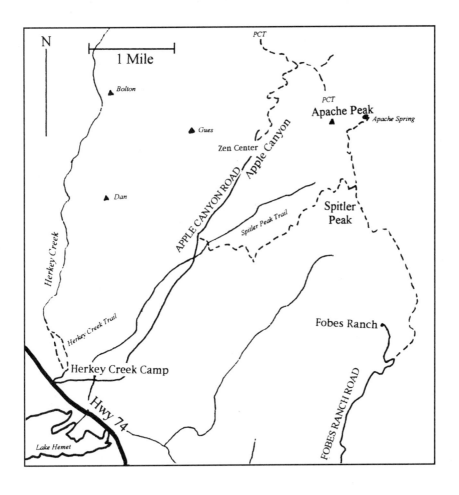

46 SOUTH RIDGE TRAIL to TAHQUITZ PEAK OVERLOOK

Length: 7 miles
Hiking Time: 4 hours
Elevation Gain: 2,000 feet
Difficulty: Strenuous

Season: May to November
Information: USDA Forest
Service, Idyllwild
(909) 659-2117

The South Ridge Trail offers the hiker access to the higher southerly elevations of the great granite massif of San Jacinto Mountain. This steep trail takes you quickly through Jeffrey pine, live oak and white fir to the more numerous lodgepole pine around Tahquitz Peak. The views, however, are the real treat. Along the way, the entire vista of the Desert Divide and Pacific Crest Trail (PCT) forming the eastern flank of the San Jacinto Mountains can be seen. To the north, the hiker sees Marion Mountain surrounded by its granite crags. This trail is steep in places and demands that the hiker be in good aerobic condition.

DIRECTIONS: This trail requires a wilderness permit from the Forest Service Office in Idyllwild (refer to the phone number above) and is reached by driving on Hwy 74 south from Hwy 111 in Palm Desert, turning right on Hwy 243 at Mountain Center and proceeding about 4 miles to Saunders Meadow Road. From I-10 in Banning, take Hwy 243 to Idyllwild and proceed south out of town until coming to this same road. Turn onto Saunders Meadow Road, then left on Pine Street for .25 mile, then right on Tahquitz View Drive for about .75 mile. You will then come to the base of South Ridge Road to the right. If you have a 4WD vehicle, proceed up the road for 1.5 mile to the trailhead; otherwise walk up to avoid the deep potholes and washouts if the winter has been severe.

Once at the trailhead, you begin a steep climb that quickly offers you those great views. After a mile you'll be able to see Garner Valley, Thomas Mountain, and Lake Hemet to the south. A little further up, the full glory of the Desert Divide Ridge is revealed to the east. Many hikers photograph themselves at a unique "window rock" found 1.5 miles up the trail and framing the wild granite crags to the north.

The trail steeply switchbacks up to Tahquitz Peak Lookout Tower, offering you a 360 degree sweep of all the mountains in this area.

View towards Tahquitz Peak and South Ridge

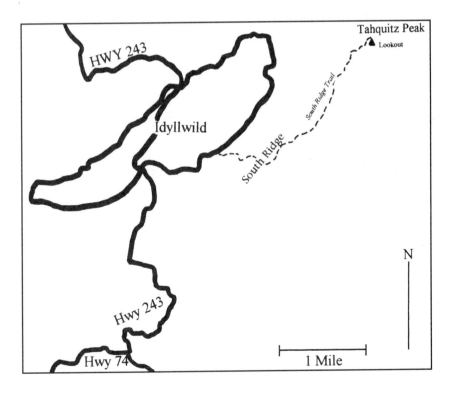

47 RAMONA TRAIL to TOOL BOX SPRING

Length: 11 miles   **Season:** Year Around
Hiking Time: 6 hours   **Information:** USDA Forest
Elevation Gain: 2,000 feet   Service, Idyllwild
Difficulty: Strenuous   (909) 659-2117

South of the San Jacinto Mountains rises the much smaller Thomas Mountain. This mountain forms the southern border for the intervening Garner Valley. There are few trails on this mountain, the San Jacintos having captured the lion's share with the Pacific Crest Trail (PCT) and Desert Divide Ridge. Still the beautiful trail to the top of Thomas Mountain via Tool Box Spring is worth the effort.

DIRECTIONS: To reach this trailhead, travel 8 miles east from the junction of Hwy 243 and 74, staying on Hwy 74 until you see the trailhead sign to your right. From Palm Desert, take Hwy 74 almost 28 miles and look for the trail sign to your left indicating Thomas Mountain.

You access the trail by walking along the dirt road, passing through a gate, then taking the trail on the left side of the road as it begins its switchback up the mountain. As is common to these mountains, you will hike through thick outgrowths of manzanita, ribbonwood and sage. Manzanita is the smooth, dark red bark bush that is often mistaken for ribbonwood, which has ribbon-like bark hanging as streamers.

After almost 3 miles you arrive at Tool Box Spring, where a dirt road joins with the trail. Continue on for another 1.5 miles west along the mountain ridge to a junction where you can turn left for the .5 mile ascent of Thomas Mountain.

The views at the top show Anza Valley to the south and the San Jacinto Mountains to the north, with Garner Valley between. This trail can be hot in the summer, depending on whether or not cool ocean breezes are blowing onshore from the Pacific.

Looking towards Thomas Mountain

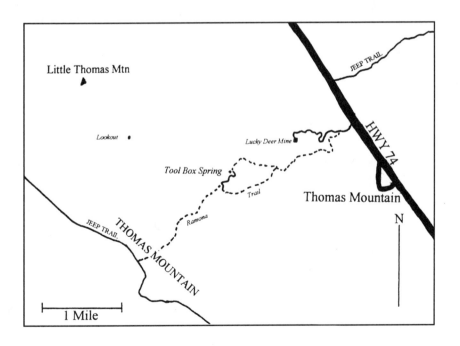

48 DEER SPRINGS TRAIL to SADDLE JUNCTION/HUMBER PARK

Length: 12 miles
Hiking Time: 7 hours
Elevation Gain: 3,300 feet
Difficulty: Strenuous

Season: May to November
Information: USDA Forest
    Service, Idyllwild
    (909) 659-2117

The Deer Springs Trail offers a vista-filled hike up San Jacinto Mountain's southwest flank, connecting to the Pacific Crest Trail (PCT), before descending along a lengthy ridge to Saddle Junction and finally Humber Park Trailhead. The views from the ridge above Idyllwild are memorable, with the massive granite Tahquitz Ridge and Lily Rock filling the southeast horizon. This is a shuttle hike requiring hikers to park cars at both the Humber Park Trailhead (Devil's Slide) and Deer Springs. The late summer weather can be tricky. The last time I did this hike we began in 80 degree temperatures and ended with a torrential downpour accompanied by hail!

> **DIRECTIONS:** To reach the trailhead for Deer Springs (Devil's Slide is described in previous hikes) take Hwy 243, 1 mile west of Idyllwild, and park on the left at the Idyllwild County Park Visitors Center. The trail begins across the street at the wooden sign.

For the first 4.1 miles, you climb through Jeffrey pine, oak and manzanita. Looking west you see Hemet Valley and Santa Anna Mountains . . . on a smog free day, that is! You then intersect the PCT, which you take up to the ridge. Along the way you are treated to beautiful views, an occasional running spring, and an excellent chance to see wildflowers, especially Indian paintbrush.

After 8.3 miles you arrive at Saddle Junction for your last 2.5 mile descent down to Humber Park. If you are shuttling, remember that on summer weekends and holidays, the Humber Park area can be filled with cars by mid morning; a day-hike permit is also required.

View towards PCT from Saddle Junction

49 SEVEN PINES TRAIL to MARION MOUNTAIN CAMP

Length: 6.5 miles
Hiking Time: 5 hours
Elevation Gain: 2,300 feet
Difficulty: Strenuous

Season: May to October
Information: USDA Forest
  Service, Idyllwild
  (909) 659-2117

This is a shuttle hike and one of the few hikes in the San Jacinto Mountains alongside a river. This trip gives the hiker great views of Fuller Ridge to the north, Hemet Valley to the west and the cooler western side of the San Jacinto Mountains. Cars need to be parked at both the Seven Pines Trailhead and the Marion Mountain Trailhead.

DIRECTIONS: From the U.S.F.S. office in Idyllwild, take Hwy 243, 5 miles west to the Allandale station, turn right for the Marion Mountain Campground and park at the trailhead just before the campground. Take the other cars back towards Hwy 243 but turn right before reaching the highway at the sign for Dark Canyon Campground. Continue through the campground and up the hill until reaching the trailhead for Seven Pines.

This trail climbs swiftly up through forest and granite boulders, with the looming, craggy wall of Fuller Ridge dominating the northern horizon. After more than a mile you are treated to the beautiful North Fork of the San Jacinto River. In early summer this river is just that. The trail crosses it through a magnificent grove of incense cedar and other pines. This makes a good rest stop and is so beautifully serene that it tempts hikers to stay and go no further. For this reason the short hike to the river makes a perfect summer picnic outing.

Hardier souls (and remember, you parked the cars at the other trailhead!) push on and upward through more lush pines and boulder outcroppings. As you climb the 2,300 feet to the junction of Marion Mountain, you crisscross a series of gullies. The trail unfortunately has been badly eroded from past runoffs and can be quite rocky and steep in places.

Once reaching the Marion Mountain Trail, turn right and down the mountain for the 2.5 mile trek back to your vehicles. The views continue to amaze, but this section of trail is especially steep, with many sections burdened by 2 foot drop-offs. Those who have done this loop prefer to travel up the river-and-fern canyons of Seven Pines Trail to avoid having to haul themselves up the steeper Marion Mountain Trail.

Many hikers are captivated by the beauty of Dark Canyon Campground they passed through to reach the Seven Pines Trailhead. The "dark" refers to the generous population of incense cedar and other thickets of pine that make this campground a welcome relief from the hotter lowlands surrounding San Jacinto Mountain.

Lake Fulmor

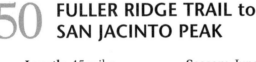

50 FULLER RIDGE TRAIL to SAN JACINTO PEAK

Length: 15 miles
Hiking Time: 10 hours
Elevation Gain: 3,200 feet
Difficulty: Strenuous

Season: June to November
Information: USDA Forest
Service, Idyllwild
(909) 659-2117

As a visitor to the Coachella Valley drives through the San Gorgonio Pass near Cabazon, they can look south to San Jacinto Peak and see a massive granite ridge emerging from the heights above the north face of San Jacinto Mountain and thrusting westward before descending sharply to the foothills beyond. This is the rugged Fuller Ridge and along its granite mass runs the Pacific Crest Trail (PCT), known through this section as the Fuller Ridge Trail. The views from near the top are magnificent, highlighting the San Gorgonio Mountains and peak to the north and the spreading deserts stretching like a carpet between the two mountain ranges. This demanding hike and its weather can be tricky. A hike has been known to begin at 7 am with 40 degree temperatures, only to end the day in the high 80's. The ascent to San Jacinto Peak further stretches your endurance, but is worth the additional effort!

DIRECTIONS: To reach the trailhead, drive 7 miles north from Idyllwild on Hwy 243 or 17 miles south from Banning on Hwy 243. Take Black Mountain Road almost 8 miles to the trailhead and park. This road, however, can be quite rough on anything but a 4WD vehicle, so plan accordingly.

From the trailhead you quickly climb to where granite outcroppings abound and the views begin to spread your horizon in all directions. After 3 to 4 miles you can look down the north face of San Jacinto Mountain into the plunging granite abyss of Snow Creek Gorge . . . this dropview alone is worth the hike! The ridge travels up and down, climbing relentlessly through pine, cedar and fir until after 5 miles the trail joins with the Deer Springs Trail. From here, turn left and proceed the 2.6 miles up to the peak of San Jacinto Mountain before returning. An easier, but more logistically difficult feat, is to have someone drop your group off at the Fuller Ridge Trailhead and instead of backtracking, continue down the eastern side of the mountain to the Mountain Tram Station and take the tram into Palm Springs before being picked up. This will shave almost 3 miles off the hike and about 1,000 feet of additional climbing.

Fuller Ridge leading to San Jacinto Mountain Peak

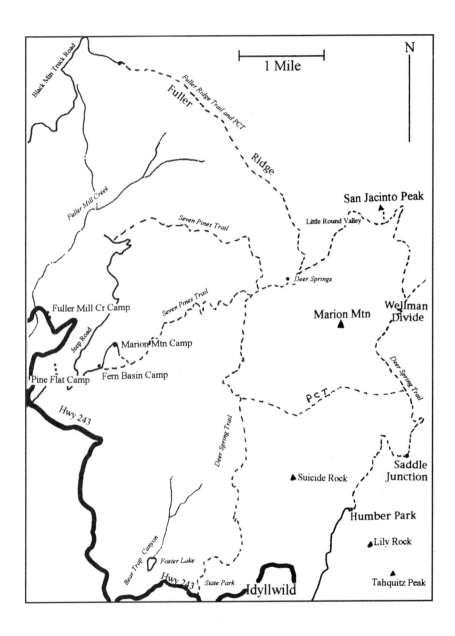

51 BLACK MOUNTAIN TRAIL

Length: 7 miles   **Season:** Year Around
Hiking Time: 4 hours   **Information:** USDA Forest
Elevation Gain: 2,600 feet   Service, Idyllwild
Difficulty: Strenuous   (909) 659-2117

This trail climbs up Black Mountain to give the hiker superb views of the desert valleys below, the Banning Pass and the San Gorgonio Mountains to the north. Black Mountain is the northern most peak in the San Jacinto Range, and one of the first hikes along the Banning-Idyllwild Road.

DIRECTIONS: To reach the trail, drive south from Banning on Hwy 243 for 13 miles until you reach Black Mountain Trail, just 1.25 miles past the Vista Grande Ranger Station.

The trail winds through a burn area left from the Soboba fire in 1974, with some charred remains still visible. After 2.5 miles you meet the Chinco Poses Trail where you continue left up the mountain before reaching the Black Mountain Lookout Road. From here hike the remaining distance to the lookout tower for vista views before returning to your starting point.

This trail can be cooler than what you might expect in summer if onshore Pacific breezes are blowing that day. For this reason, this trail is a favorite with desert hikers seeking to cool off without driving all the way to Idyllwild.

*Black
Mountain*

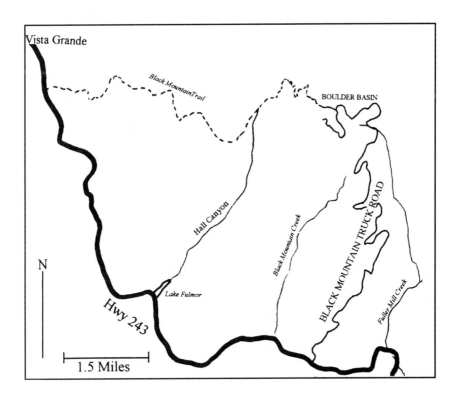

52 NORTH FORK of the PCT to LIVE OAK SPRING

Length: 14 miles
Hiking Time: 8 hours
Elevation Gain: 2,000 feet
Difficulty: Strenuous

Season: Year Around
Information: USDA Forest
　　Service, Idyllwild
　　(909) 659-2117

The North Fork of the Pacific Crest Trail (PCT) offers the hiker a scenic, meandering, gradual climb to the Desert Divide Ridge overlooking the Coachella Valley with the added treat of visiting a beautiful grove of massive oak trees surrounded by grassy meadows and vine thickets, all fed by the rushing water of Live Oak Spring. The Desert Divide Ridge is accompanied all the way to Idyllwild by the PCT. It offers a cool escape from the sweltering desert below and stunning vistas of the Coachella Valley, Santa Rosa and San Jacinto Mountain Ranges and the Salton Sea Basin on the eastern horizon.

DIRECTIONS: The trailhead directions are the same as the South Fork PCT, taking Hwy 74 from Palm Desert 23 miles to the parking area, or .5 mile east of the Hwy 371 junction.

The trail begins with a massive mileage sign and description of the PCT system found in this area. The trail winds slowly down a hillside covered with manzanita, yucca, juniper and pine. While not terribly spectacular vista-wise, the scents are invigorating in the cool morning air. The trail makes its way into a boulder area for several miles, then climbs alongside a low mountain. The views show working ranches below as well as the Mount Palomar Observatory to the southwest. You pass through a variety of pine and high desert scrub brush, with some small streams running from January to March.

After 5 miles the trail crosses a small dirt road. Look for the rock ducks that indicate the trail continuing on the other side of this road. You now hug a rocky mountainside for the last mile before reaching the top of the trail at Desert Divide. This is exactly 6 miles from where you began. Continue down for another mile to Live Oak Spring. The spring area offers a quiet and green lunch stop. It reminds many hikers of the oak covered hillsides in Northern California. The two oak tree systems found at Live Oak Spring are massive due to the perpetual source of running water. If you continued 5 miles down the mountain you would intersect Palm Canyon.

Take care to bring enough cold water. In these parts you often begin a hike with cool temperatures but end the afternoon pushing 90 to 100 degrees.

Monument trail marker for north fork of the PCT

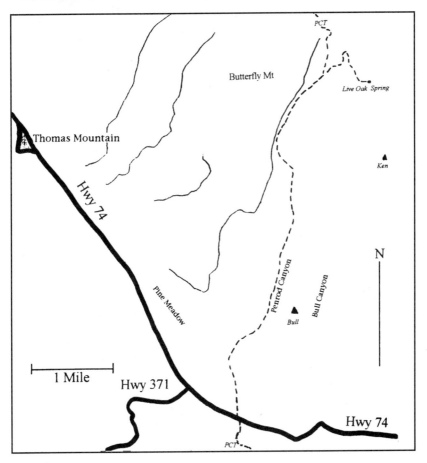

SANTA ROSA MOUNTAINS

53 HORSETHIEF CREEK via CACTUS SPRING TRAIL

Length: 5 miles
Hiking Time: 4 hours
Elevation Gain: 900 feet
Difficulty: Easy/Moderate

Season: October to May
Information: USDA Forest
Service, Idyllwild
(909) 659-2117

The Santa Rosa Mountain Wilderness area is a world apart from the desert surrounding it. This is a land of high chaparral, pinyon pine, yucca, juniper, agave, manzanita, ribbonwood and prickly pear. The southern horizon is dominated by the twin massifs of Santa Rosa and Toro Peaks, 8,000 and 8,700 feet high, while to the northwest the hiker can see the San Jacinto and San Gorgonio mountains filling up the western sky. A favorite and easy way to explore this wild country is to hike the length of the Cactus Spring Trail that penetrates deep into this wilderness area. The first segment of this hike is the beautiful Horsethief Creek section.

DIRECTIONS: To reach the trailhead, turn south from Hwy 111 in Palm Desert onto Hwy 74. Proceed up the mountain for almost 16 miles until you pass Sugarloaf Cafe where you will take the first paved road to the left. A sign on Hwy 74 indicates the Cactus Spring Trailhead. Go .25 mile then turn left onto the wide dirt road. Park in the flat area north of the trash disposal. From Hemet, the trailhead is 8 miles east of the junction of Hwy 371 and Hwy 74.

After parking, hike east down the dirt road, then right (south) when you come to the larger dirt road heading up the mountain. After 100 yards you will see Cactus Spring Trail sign to the left. Begin down the trail and be careful to turn as it veers right after .25 mile. You will begin making your way through a thicket of vegetation, cactus and pinyon pine. Within minutes the trail opens onto the remains of an abandoned dolomite mine. Continue east. The trail is a roller coaster, up and down journey with a bias to the down side. Be careful of fine loose rock when heading downhill. Sturdy hiking boots will help cushion this rocky trail.

While you head east Martinez Mountain fills the horizon. The trail is often washed by several streams and caution must be taken against slippery rocks. By April most of the streams have dried up. Hikers are amazed by the large size of plants, made so by the abundant runoff during the winter.

After more than 2 miles, look to your left for the remains of an old corral made of dried manzanita. Cowboys once kept their herds penned there due to the water supply of Horsethief Creek. It will be slightly downhill and off-trail.

The trail brings you to a rise above Horsethief Creek in a dramatic fashion. From this vantage point you can view the beautiful cottonwood and sycamore trees lining the creek bed for the better part of a mile. In late October, the canyon creek area is ablaze with bright yellow and suggests a scene more from Pennsylvania than a California wilderness. Drop down into the creek and you can explore upstream for a mile, although there is no trail to lead you . . . just follow the water through thickets of vines, trees and bushes. Many hikers come to Horsethief Creek for a reprieve from the sweltering desert heat below, and are well rewarded. After returning to their vehicles, many hikers opt for a visit to Sugarloaf Cafe, where they will find friendly service, good food and a pleasant atmosphere.

Horsethief Creek. Photo by Sue Bobek

Looking towards trail's end at Sugarloaf Mountain

 # 54 CACTUS SPRING TRAIL

Length: 9 miles
Hiking Time: 5 hours
Elevation Gain: 1,200 feet
Difficulty: Moderate

Season: October to May
Information: USDA Forest
Service, Idyllwild
(909) 659-2117

The trail to Cactus Spring brings the hiker into even closer contact with the Santa Rosa Wilderness. This a continuation hike from Horsethief Creek, traveling an additional 2 miles to a spring that unfortunately is often dry. Still, this trail provides some scenic vistas of Martinez Mountain and chaparral covered slopes of the vast watershed known as Horsethief Creek. If the winter rains have been abundant, then the hiker is treated to a scattering of mini-waterfalls cascading from the northern face of the Santa Rosa Mountains which form the boundary of the hiker's southern horizon.

DIRECTIONS: Directions to this trailhead is provided in the hike description of Horsethief Creek.

The trail continues on the eastern side of the creek with a steep climb up a sometimes slippery slope. You reach the top after climbing 400 feet and can then see the wide mountain vistas of the Horsethief Creek basin. After .25 mile on the top you drop down into a delightful, small canyon that slowly winds itself ever higher and deeper into the wilderness. Sometimes a stream runs the length of this wash, and helps nurture the abundant plant life.

The trail emerges from the canyon through a dense thicket of juniper and pinyon pine. It follows the wooden post trail markers onto a level plateau. Here, the spacious views allow you to see the wilderness area, hidden from the desert dwellers below by the cover of the lower foothills. Martinez Mountain grows ever larger as you approach Cactus Spring. You know you're there when to your left you see a dense cover of grasses flowing down into the wash. Other than that, in the dry season Cactus Spring is that in name only.

I have been especially fond of this hike because of the clean, crisp air, heavily scented with juniper and pine mixed with the more arid desert plants. The feel of the hike along the final mile is expansive, energizing and wild, with the wilderness showing no signs of human presence and the sprawl of the Coachella Valley below is completely hidden from view. October and March seem to be the best time weather-wise, with early spring offering the hiker plenty of blooming cactus and wildflowers.

Martinez Mountain from Cactus Spring Trailhead

55 AGUA ALTA SPRING

Length: 18 miles
Hiking Time: 11 hours
Elevation Gain: 2,400 feet
Difficulty: Strenuous

Season: October to April
Information: USDA Forest
Service, Idyllwild
(909) 659-2117

The trail to Agua Alta Spring is the last of the Cactus Spring Trail that can be hiked in a day, be it a strenuous, and a long one. This segment takes the hiker into the furthest reaches of the Santa Rosa Wilderness. It conjures up images and feelings of a forgotten past, when the Cahuilla Indians roamed the canyons and slopes surrounding Martinez Mountain, gathering pinyon pine nuts and edible cactus, while surviving the harsh Sonoran desert lifestyle. The views in the recesses of upper Martinez Canyon are ones of desolate slopes, sheer rocky canyon walls, and the searing desert floor in the distance. It is a journey worth the taking, and challenges the hiker's inner spirits to make peace with the empty stillness of this unique wilderness environment.

DIRECTIONS: The trailhead is the same as Horsethief Creek and Cactus Spring.

You continue from Cactus Spring, heading left into the large wash and following the wooden post trail markers. After more than a mile, the trail turns slowly right and winds its way up towards the saddle that separates Martinez Mountain from Horsethief Creek Basin.

The trail continues down through several dry washes. Magnificent views of the surrounding canyons awe the hiker as well as the 6,500 foot Martinez Mountain filling the view to the left. At any rate, in the vicinity of the southern back side of this mountain you can choose to climb to its top, but there is no trail and the rock scrambling can exhaust all but the hardiest hiker. If you continue past Martinez Mountain you will reach Agua Alta Springs at a point 6 miles from Horsethief Creek. This trail section is faint in places and requires some bushwhacking. The hike back to the trailhead is long and hot in the late spring, so at least 4 quarts of water is suggested. Once finished, the hiker can seek refreshments at the Sugarloaf Cafe.

Santa Rosa from Cactus Spring Trail
Photo by Sue Bobek

Saddle west of Agua Alta

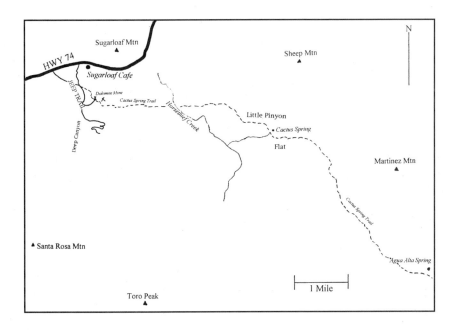

## 56 ROCKHOUSE CANYON TRAIL

Length: 16 miles
Hiking Time: 9 hours
Elevation Gain: 2,000 feet
Difficulty: Very strenuous

Season: October to April
Information: BLM Office
Palm Springs
(619) 251-4800

Rockhouse Canyon Trail is a combination canyon/trail and dirt trail that takes the adventurous hiker deep into the backcountry of the lower Santa Rosa Mountains and the Martinez Canyon area. This is a designated wilderness area, so the once 6 mile jeep drive to the trailhead has been cut back to about 3.5 miles due to the exclusion of motorized travel once you cross over into wilderness area.

The hike follows a stream during the winter/spring and eventually makes its way onto a low foothill, from where you get fabulous views of the soaring canyons and surrounding mountains hemming you in on all sides. The payoff at trail's end is the Jack Miller rock cabin, well preserved, with BLM historical data and artifacts accenting the rugged setting of this backcountry pioneer home. This trail or route should only be taken with someone who knows the way and has actually been to the rockhouse. More than one hiker has lost the trail searching for the elusive "rockhouse."

DIRECTIONS: Take Hwy 111 through Indio and turn right (south) onto Jackson Street, traveling 5 miles to Avenue 66. From this corner, head to the right on the 4WD jeep road, on private land, following it up a small ridge. To the left are citrus groves, while brittle bush and desert vegetation fill the washes all the way to the surrounding mountains. Stay on the ridge for 1.2 miles, turn right off the ridge and follow the jeep road alongside the mountains. After about 3.5 miles from Avenue 66 you cross into BLM Wilderness Land. Park your jeep or 4WD vehicle and begin hiking past the beautiful ocotillo field to the south.

Head towards Martinez Canyon, in a westerly direction, keeping your eye ahead to Toro Peak. This trail is very rocky and taxes the leg strength of even the most determined hiker. You eventually reach a stream. Keep on the north side to take advantage of the remnants of the old jeep road built by Miller.

The canyon narrows, requires some bushwhacking, but takes you into a gorgeous water chute falls. This area is deep with water, and some hikers remove their boots to negotiate the falls.

Continue up the canyon, through an area thick with cottonwood trees. Just .75 mile from here is the rockhouse. The views are beautiful from the cabin's front door and offers hikers a comfortable resting place before their strenuous return down canyon.

Jack Miller's Rockhouse

Ocotillo field near the entrance of Martinez Canyon

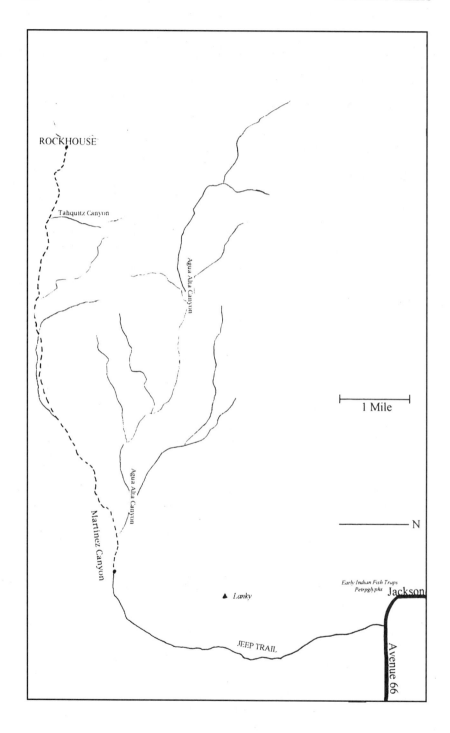

ROCKHOUSE

Tahquitz Canyon

Agua Alta Canyon

1 Mile

Agua Alta Canyon

N

Martinez Canyon

Early Indian Fish Traps
Petrpglyphs   Jackson

▲ Lanky

JEEP TRAIL

Avenue 66

57 SANTA ROSA MOUNTAIN ROAD to TORO PEAK

Length: 3 miles
Hiking Time: 2 hours
Elevation Gain: 800 feet
Difficulty: Easy

Season: May to November
Information: USDA Forest
Service, Idyllwild
(909) 659-2117

The climb to Toro Peak is a short 800 feet elevation gain, but with a spectacular vista payoff. At 8,716 feet, Toro Peak dominates the Santa Rosa Mountain Range. The stunning views from the top encompass the entire east-to-west Santa Rosa Mountains, the Coachella Valley and Salton Sea, the San Jacinto Mountains to the west, and the sprawling Anza Borrego State Park and deserts reaching all the way to Mexico. Toro Peak, however, is no longer the wilderness destination it once was. The Marine Corps has laid claim to the peak by building a radio-relay/TV microwave station on the summit.

DIRECTIONS: To reach the trailhead, drive south on Hwy 74 from Palm Desert and Hwy 111, 20 miles to the Santa Rosa Mountain Road. This is a "dirt road," suitable for 4WD vehicles, and after a rough winter, can be brutal, with large potholes and eroded gullies. After driving almost 12 miles you encounter a locked gate. Park where convenient, so as not to block other traffic.

The trail is actually the road past the locked gate, and continues up for almost 1.25 miles. At the road fork, turn right and climb the very steep remaining roadway to the summit.

The vistas are outstanding, giving you a good feel for this peak being a true "island-in-the-sky." You can explore the summit area, bushwhack to any interesting nearby destinations and eventually backtrack to your vehicle.

Rattlesnake. Photo by Sue Bobek

58 SAWMILL ROAD TRAIL

Length: 8 miles   **Season:** March to November
Hiking Time: 5 hours   **Information:** USDA Forest
Elevation Gain: 2,500 feet   Service, Idyllwild
Difficulty: Strenuous   (909) 659-2117

The Sawmill Road Trail currently provides the only access up the north facing slope of Toro Peak and the Santa Rosa Mountains. At the time of this book printing, plans are in effect for building a connector trail from the end of Sawmill Road to the Santa Rosa Peak Trail system at the top of the mountains. As it currently stands, this trail falls short of the peak, and the steep pine-covered slopes of upper Santa Rosa Mountain prevent any comfortable bushwhacking attempt to reach the top. Check with the Forest Service in Idyllwild to see if the connector trail has been completed.

> **DIRECTIONS:** To reach the current trailhead, follow the directions given for Horsethief Creek Trail. After heading east from the parking area, the hiker connects to a large dirt road heading up the mountain, This is Sawmill Road Trail.

The trail road winds relentlessly up the mountain. As it does, it gives the hiker magnificent vistas of the Santa Rosa-San Jacinto Mountain chain, the Coachella Valley below, and perhaps the only good view of the impressive Deep Canyon that bordered Hwy 74 to the east all the way up to Sugarloaf Cafe. For many, Sawmill Road presents a quick ascent into the cooler pine forests near Santa Rosa Peak, gives you a great exercise/cardiovascular workout, and as previously mentioned, will provide a thoroughfare to the peak once the trail is extended.

There is no shade or cover of any kind on this trail until you reach the first pine trees almost at the trail's finish. Still, this is a worthy hike considering the vistas and the great exercise.

Sawmill Road Trail reaching towards Santa Rosa Mountain

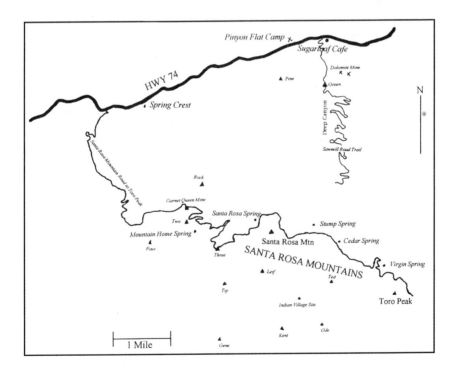

59 PALM CANYON PINES-to-PALMS TRAIL

Length: 16 miles
Hiking Time: 8 hours
Elevation Loss: 3,200 feet
Difficulty: Strenuous

Season: October to April
Information: USDA Forest
    Service, Idyllwild
    (909) 659-2117

This is a 5-star hike, a must for serious hikers wanting to visit, in one day, flora and fauna ranging from Canadian type pine to Mexico's Sonoran deserts. The time of year is critical for doing this hike. It may start out at the top (4,000 feet) cool if not cold, but end in the lower reaches of Palm Canyon's desert area (800 feet) in blistering heat of 90+ degrees. This hike is also best taken with hikers who have done the trail before, and should not be attempted alone. This is because the trail follows much of Palm Canyon's sandy bottom, exits at places easy to miss and can be washed out or seriously eroded if the winter rains have been heavy. In 1994 a fire ravaged the entire area, burning almost 5 miles of this 16 mile hike. This further eroded what was once a well-maintained trail used by both hikers and mountain bikers.

> **DIRECTIONS:** To reach the trailhead, turn south onto Hwy 74 from Hwy 111 in Palm Desert. After 18 miles you reach the Ribbonwood area. Turn to your right at Pine View Drive and proceed to its end, .25 mile from the highway. At the time of printing this book, the Forest Service is planning another trailhead that will originate in the Pinyon Flats Campground. Check with them for changed trailhead directions.

After parking, begin hiking down the road and veer right when you see the small sign indicating "riding trail." Even if you miss this, the trail is an obvious downgrade along the ridge of the mountain. For the next several miles you encounter mesquite, sage, yucca, pinyon and juniper pines. The views are fantastic looking north, west and east. A valley of mountains sprawls before you in all directions and you get a clear over-view of the Palm Canyon watershed plunging into the long, deepening form of the canyon, itself.

After 3 miles, you drop down into Palm Canyon from the ridge. Along the way the hiker sees a sign indicating a ridge route. Take this ridge route to avoid dropping into the canyon too early. Once in the canyon follow the wash to the left where it joins up with the main canyon. A quick climb over a small hill will reveal a beautiful stand of cottonwood often brilliant yellow in early November.

When you reach the main body of Palm Canyon, turn right and follow the combination wash and trail. Stay always on the right side of the canyon. Over the next several miles you will do many 10- to 20-foot climbs above the canyon, then drop down again. Eventually you see a rock duck on the right side of the canyon where you will again climb out but stay above the canyon for several miles. This trail continues through washes, and up the canyon side for several more miles until you reach the sign indicating Live Oak Spring. The trail then continues up the right side of the canyon. You can measure your distance easy enough by noting the mileage markers that tell how far you are from Hwy 74. After the marker says 6 miles, and you continue for another 2 miles or so, look for the mountains to the west to begin forming some steep drops into Palm Canyon. In this section of the hike, the canyon narrows and deepens. Water in late winter rushes through the rocky gorges and several waterfalls grace the slopes above the canyon. This area is known as Upper Paradise and makes a good lunch stop. Trees and pools of water are abundant, with the first fan palms now beginning to appear. From this point, the Indian Trading Post in Palm Canyon, the northern end of this spectacular hike, is only three hours away.

As the trail continues towards Palm Springs, the San Jacinto Mountains increase in size and dominate the western view. You are literally hiking through a valley of mountains. The trail connects with a wash that takes you several miles until you see another rock duck to your right. You will know you are at this junction because the trail dropping down from the right continues across the wash and to the left. Take the trail up the right side of the hill and continue the last several miles until you finally drop down into the thick grove of Washingtonian palms that give Palm Canyon its name. You are now just a mile from the trading post. Wind your way to the left while staying right of the stream. The trail follows the stream, veers right and passes a large side canyon on your left. Stay right, cross the stream where safe, and follow the trail to the trading post. You have just finished an all-day adventure that for many opens up the natural wonders and beauty of this desert playground like nothing else they can ever do. I suggest any hiker unfamiliar with the trail contact the Coachella Valley Hiking Club at (619) 345-6234. This

View at Little Paradise

hiking group does the Pines-to-Palms trail twice a year and will gladly furnish you with any information you need. To make this hike in one day, have someone drop you off at the upper trailhead on Hwy 74 and pick you up at the trading post in Palm Canyon (also known as Hermit's Bench). If you are a strong hiker and begin hiking at 7 am you will reach the Indian trading post no later than 3 to 4 pm.

Cliff overlooks of Palm Canyon Trail

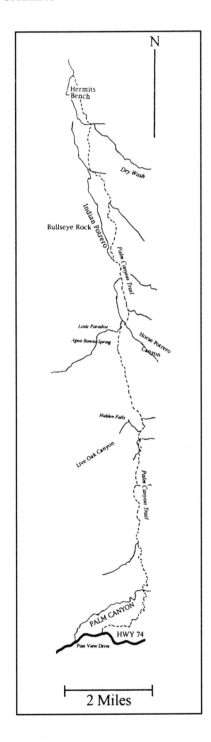

60 SOUTH FORK of the PACIFIC CREST TRAIL (PCT)

Length: 11 miles
Hiking Time: 6 hours
Elevation Gain: 800 feet
Difficulty: Strenuous

Season: September to May
Information: USDA Forest
    Service, Idyllwild
    (909) 659-2117

The Pacific Crest Trail (PCT) is the western answer to the eastern Appalachian Trail. Each runs south to north along the predominate mountain ranges found inland from both oceans. Both are over 2,000 miles in length. The PCT crosses near the Coachella Valley at the junction of Hwy 74 and Hwy 371 in Garner Valley. The trail reaches out and climbs to the ridge above the desert known as the Desert Divide, proceeds west along the ridge to the mountains above Idyllwild, drops down the northwest side of San Jacinto Mountain and into the Banning Pass, crossing over I-10 before heading north towards the Big Bear/ Lake Arrowhead area. The south fork is that section heading south towards Mexico, where the PCT meets Hwy 74. It is a world apart from the North Fork, just across the highway, tending to be much warmer and desert-like.

DIRECTIONS: To reach the trailhead for both the South and North Fork, take Hwy 74 out of Palm Desert (south at the Hwy 111 junction) and proceed 23 miles, or from Hemet drive .5 mile east of the Hwy 371 junction. There is a PCT sign on the right indicating a parking area. Park and cross the highway to the south, where you will come to a gate that opens onto the trail. The sign here indicates mileage south of this point. The South Fork as described here goes .75 mile beyond Table Mountain Road.

The trail first takes you through sage and low brush, up a mountainside and along a low ridge. From here you can see the mountainous terrain that makes up the northern PCT route, and the magnificent vista of San Jacinto Mountain. The trail swings alongside the mountain for 2 miles. To the left you eventually see a steep canyon network that marks the northern watershed for the Anza Borrego Desert, 20 miles to the southeast. You also glimpse row after row of distant mountain ranges, while to the right, low hills rise whose deep green winter color suggests a hike in Wales. Passing through a flat meadow area, the trail begins a series of up and down wash crossings and alternating hill climbs. To the east this hike shows you the best view of Santa Rosa Mountain's southwestern flank.

After 4.5 miles the PCT reaches Table Mountain Road. Continue on for another .75 mile for a great view of the Anza Valley. More importantly, in late March and early April the trail turn-around point is a field of brilliant golden California poppies that serves as a colorful and restful lunch stop. Please note the weather conditions, as this trail can get very hot (100 degrees) in September or April if no Pacific inland winds are blowing.

Mount San Jacinto from Pacific Crest Trailhead

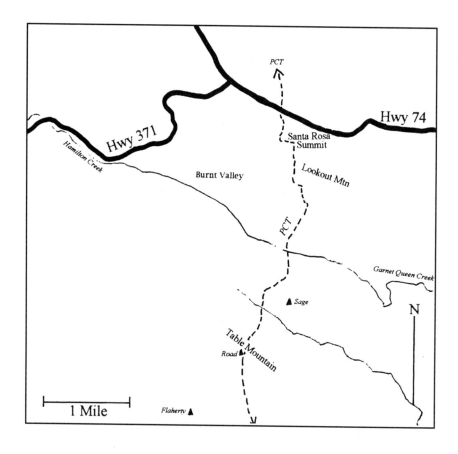

JOSHUA TREE NATIONAL PARK

61 LONG CANYON to CHUCKAWALLA BILL'S RUINS

Length: 12 miles
Hiking Time: 6 hours
Elevation Gain: 1,800 feet
Difficulty: Strenuous

Season: October to May
Information: BLM Office
Palm Springs
(619) 251-4800

This hike takes you from the Joshua Tree National Park area through the interesting, scenic Long Canyon and finally to the remains of Chuckawalla Bill's roofless stone cabin. The hike through the wash can be quite tiring wherever you reach sand, although much of this trail is on hard wash bottom, so be sure to bring enough cool water and food.

DIRECTIONS: To begin this hike, drive west on I-10 to Hwy 62, turn and travel north until reaching Yucca Valley. There, turn right on Joshua Lane, right at Warren Vista, until reaching the corner of Andreas Road. The pavement ends here and a 4WD vehicle is recommended (high clearance). Turn right onto the dirt road for .5 mile, then left onto the next dirt road (after 1.2 miles you see a barbed wire fence indicating National Park boundary). Proceed another .5 mile, turn left and go up the road towards the radio tower. Park after .3 mile at a row of 5 metal culverts beside a stone drainage ditch.

Head south 100 yards to the trailhead, down about .5 mile of rocky trail, down over a 15 foot rock scramble and on into the bottom of Long Canyon Wash. There are many side washes but this does not pose a problem when you head down the main wash in a southern direction, if you mark your way with arrows and rocks for your return to the trailhead. Continue south, down Long Canyon Wash to reach Chuckawalla Bill Wash.

The distant Santa Rosa Mountains, to the south, assist you in finding your way. You eventually pass through a slick rock chute where shortly the Santa Rosa Mountains become visible before disappearing, then re-appearing at the point where the wash widens. Here, vehicle tracks are often seen, and the Joshua trees thin out dramatically. 1.5 miles from the rock chute, on the left side is a 2 foot rock cairn while on the right side the earth has been washed away from the hillside, exposing rusty brown soil and rocks. This wash heading west takes you to Chuckawalla Bill's cabin.

You will find scattered metal and wood pieces in the wash as you walk up to the roofless, stone cabin. There is a spring about 100 yards past the cabin which is visible after a wet spell.

This is an interesting "wilderness" type hike, but first time hikers might think of going with someone familiar with the trail and all its intricacies.

Remains of Chuckawalla Bill's home

62 EUREKA PEAK LOOP

Length: 10 miles
Hiking Time: 6 hours
Elevation Gain: 1,500 feet
Difficulty: Strenuous

Season: September to May
Information: Joshua Tree
National Park
Twentynine
Palms
(619) 367-7511

Eureka Peak, at 5,518 feet, commands a dominating view of the western boundary of Joshua Tree National Park, including the lower Coachella Valley, San Jacinto Mountain, and San Gorgonio Peak. For this reason it is well worth the effort of struggling up sandy washes and over steep ridges to gain the heights and subsequent views afforded by Eureka Peak. The hike itself shows the flora of high desert (4,000 to 5,000 feet) in a myriad of small canyons and washes leading up to the peak. In spring the hiker is treated to cooler temperatures verses the searing heat below, and the vegetation after a wet winter is abundantly green.

DIRECTIONS: Begin this hike by driving from I-10 to Hwy 62, north into Yucca Valley. Just past Yucca Valley take the road to the right, Joshua Lane, at the junction with Hwy 247 and continue into Black Rock Canyon Visitor's Center. The trail begins north of the visitor's center, east of the parking area.

The trail sign at this point indicates the California Riding and Hiking Trail, marked by brown posts. Stay on this trail for 2 miles until the trail enters a large wash and forks. Take the right fork (south) marked by an orange post. In about .5 mile the wash forks again. Take the small wash right, to where it ends at a small gully. Another orange marking post will direct you to the left for a climb over a ridge. From here, head to the right in a south by southeast direction up to a saddle and around the south side of Eureka Peak, almost 5 miles from your starting point. Even if the trail appears poorly marked, tracks from previous hikes help you find your way.

To return, after taking in the wonderful views from the top, head east and down perhaps .5 mile until reaching the junction with the California Riding and Hiking Trail. Turn left and follow this trail all the way back to your starting point. The route is mainly flat and down, through a series of washes and small valleys. It's a good idea to inquire at the Visitor's Center as to the condition of the trail and any improvements made in marking it.

Cholla cactus grove in Joshua Tree National Park

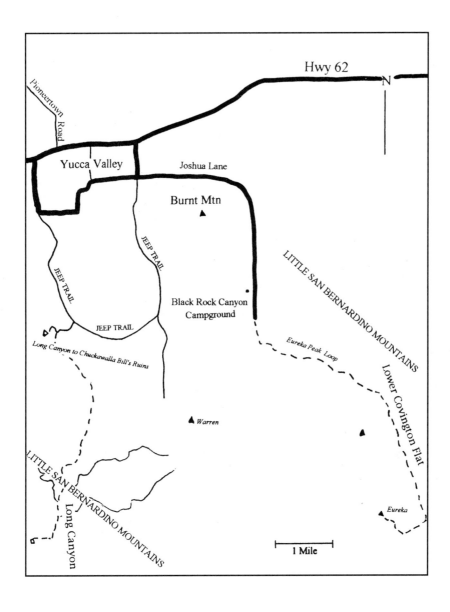

63 COVINGTON LOOP TRAIL

Length: 6 miles
Hiking Time: 4 hours
Elevation Gain: 400 feet
Difficulty: Moderate

Season: October to June
Information: Joshua Tree
   National Park
   Twentynine Palms
   (619) 367-7511

The Covington Loop Trail is an easy but scenic introduction to the backcountry of Joshua Tree National Park. This hike makes a loop through Lower and Upper Covington Flats, past the largest Joshua Tree in the National Park, with a good offering of high desert vegetation, including juniper, yucca and pinyon.

DIRECTIONS: From Palm Springs, drive west to Hwy 62, turn right and head north 25 miles to Yucca Valley and La Contena Road. Turn right at La Contena, going to the end of the pavement at La Contena and Yucca. Continue south on the dirt jeep road 1.75 miles to the Covington Flat Area sign, turn left in a southerly direction for 9 miles, following the National Park signs for the picnic area and the Backcountry Trailhead.

From the trailhead at the backcountry sign, head northeast through the wash and down the canyon. When you join the Lower Covington Flats Trail, head northwest up the trail to the picnic area. At the picnic area follow the route southeast to a Y and go right. Left takes you to a small abandoned mine. The brown trail markers assist the hiker with arrows pointing the way.

At 2 miles from the picnic area, the trail joins the California Riding and Hiking Trail (CRH). Follow this trail back to Upper Covington Flats. During the loop hike you will pass an obviously very large Joshua Tree . . . the largest in the park. It is over 35 feet high and 17 feet round at the base. In recent years it has shown signs of wind damage and dead limbs.

Largest Joshua Tree in the Park found just off the Covington Loop Trail

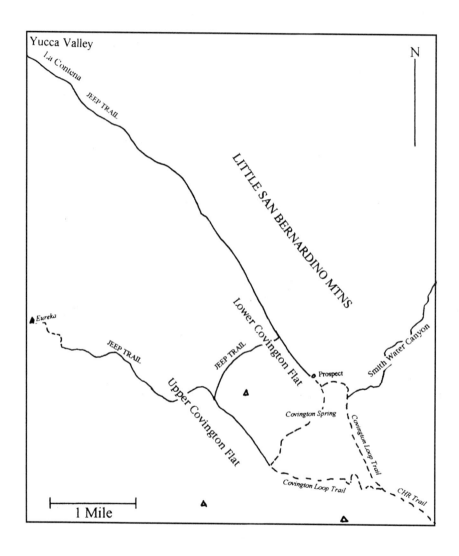

 # 64 BARKER DAM LOOP

Length: 1.5 miles
Hiking Time: 2 hours
Elevation Gain: 0
Difficulty: Easy

Season: October to June
Information: Joshua Tree
National Park
Twentynine Palms
(619) 367-7511

Joshua Tree National Park is a maze of huge boulders, uplifted mountains and exotic high mountain desert plants. One of the key areas in the Park for viewing the sometimes strange and unique rock formations is the Wonderland of Rocks, where a man-made dam has captured water runoff and created a small but unique lake. The area boasts of interesting boulder formations and the hike, while short, makes a good diversion from the more strenuous hikes the Park has to offer.

DIRECTIONS: To reach the Wonderland of Rocks area, take Hwy 62 off I-10, north to Joshua Tree. Continue through town until coming to the turnoff to the right for the Park Entrance. Once at the fee station, drive another 10 miles to the Hidden Valley Campground where a dirt road leads you another 2 miles to the Barker Dam parking area.

From north of the parking area take the signed interpretive trail, highlighting the local desert plant life, into the Wonderland of Rocks. The trail leads into the Barker Dam area, where it meanders along the lake. From here explore whatever strikes your interest before returning.

Barker Dam

*Petroglyphs on the Barker
Dam Loop*

65 RYAN MOUNTAIN TRAIL

Length: 4 mile
Hiking Time: 3 hours
Elevation Gain: 700 feet
Difficulty: Moderate

Season: October to May
Information: Joshua Tree
National Park
Twentynine Palms
(619) 367-7511

The top of Ryan Mountain offers one of the best circular views of the surrounding scenic features found in Joshua National Park. The views include the high summit peaks of San Jacinto Mountain and San Gorgonio, Pinto Basin, Lost Horse Valley, the Wonderland of Rocks, and the Little San Bernardino Mountains, forming the northern border of the Coachella Valley. The trail is well maintained, considered a moderate hike, but if taken at a slow pace, can be done as an easy hike.

DIRECTIONS: To begin, drive south 3 miles on Utah Trail Road from the Joshua Tree National Park Visitor's Center at Twentynine Palms. Stay right at the Pinto Y junction for 8 miles until reaching the Sheep Pass Campground on your left, where you will park.

The trail begins from the campground with immediate views of massive boulders and Joshua trees. The climb up to Ryan Peak (5,470 feet) allows you to begin seeing the spreading valleys below, but the real vistas are reserved for the top, as the 360 degree views fill every horizon.

*Ryan Mountain
Trailhead*

 # 66 LOST HORSE MINE LOOP

Length: 8 miles
Hiking Time: 4 hours
Elevation Gain: 600 feet
Difficulty: Moderate

Season: September to June
Information: Joshua Tree
National Park
Twentynine Palms
(619) 367-7511

Located near the center of the National Park, the Lost Horse Mine Loop Trail combines three hikes in one, giving hikers a visit to a once success-ful working gold mine, some of the most spectacular desert-mountain vistas in Southern California, and a delightful meander through a gentle wash generously filled with Joshua trees, yucca, juniper and a host of other representative high desert plants. Add to these the views looking south towards the Coachella Valley and you have the making of a really fine day-hike that introduces you to the stunning natural beauty of Joshua Tree National Park.

DIRECTIONS: To begin this hiking adventure, drive north on Hwy 62, off I-10, just a few miles west of Palm Springs. Continue north into the town of Joshua Tree where you will turn right at the sign indicat-ing the Joshua Tree National Park entrance (Park Blvd.). Continue through a sparse scattering of homes until reaching the Park Entrance. After paying the fee, continue through the Park to Caprock Junction, where you will turn right onto Keyes Road for another 2.5 miles. On the left, look for the dirt road directing you to Lost Horse Mine.

After parking, begin hiking the trail found east of the parking lot and starting just past the interpretive display. The trail takes you up for 2 miles until reaching your first destination, the Lost Horse Mine. Ex-plore the remains and read the description of what the operation of this mine entailed. Continue on the same trail that got you to the mine, but know that from this point there will be few hikers, as most choose to reach the mine and return to their vehicles before pushing on to another destination in the Park.

In less than .5 mile from the mine the trail climbs to a series of fantastic overlooks into Lost Horse, Queen and Pleasant Valleys, and even to the distant, jagged Coxcomb Mountains, marking the furthest eastern boundary of the Park.

The park begins a descent along a ridge and gives you a good feel for the rugged desert mountain environment. In less than a mile you come to a large hole that marks a once used mine shaft. Continue hiking, noting a series of rock cairns along the right side of the trail. From the large hole, travel about .25 mile until you see both a rock cairn to your right and a low saddle about 100 feet above you. Leave the trail at this point, rock scrambling up the slope to the top. From there head south by southwest down and sometimes over low ridges until you see, at 40 to 100 yards beneath you, the remains of a tall, stone fireplace. Hike down to this area and explore what's left of a prospector's once proud home. The trail picks up just west of the fireplace, and the distance from where you left the main trial is no more than .5 mile. If finding this part of the Lost Horse Mine Loop Trail proves too difficult, backtrack to the main trail and return to your vehicle by hiking past the mine and down the mountain.

If you are successful in connecting with the loop via the fireplace remains, continue on the trail, climbing to a wonderful plateau offering great views of the Santa Rosa Mountains and San Jacinto Peak. In another mile you will reach a turn to the right, marked by rock cairns, after exiting a short, dry wash. For the next 1.5 miles you will be hiking through a flat but delightful valley, making your way over sandy trails but marked sporadically by cairns. This section of trail takes you directly back to the parking lot . . . you will find that the trail bears right at any junction and keeps you in a desert wash bordered on both sides by low mountains.

Lost Horse Mine

Remains of a prospector's once proud home

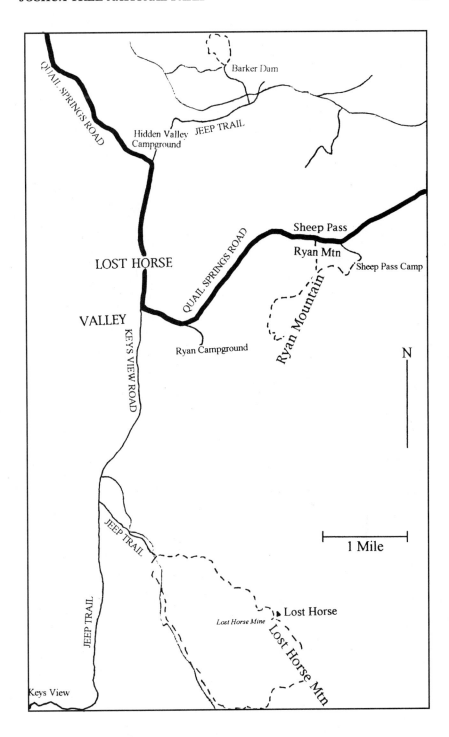

67 LOST PALMS OASIS TRAIL at COTTONWOOD SPRING

Length: 8 miles
Hiking Time: 4 hours
Elevation Gain: 400 feet
Difficulty: Moderate

Season: September to May
Information: Joshua Tree
National Park
Twentynine Palms
(619) 367-7511

On the southernmost boundary of Joshua Tree National Park several minor earthquake fault lines, branches of the San Andreas fault line 20 miles southwest, cut through the low mountains overlooking I-10. By so doing, the fault encourages water to seep to the surface. At one such point a large, lush growth of California fan palms can be explored and admired for their stately beauty. This particular grouping of fan palms has come to be known as Lost Palms Oasis, and makes a beautiful day-hike through washes, over plateaus, offering stunning views of the surrounding mountains and valleys, including the distant San Jacinto Mountain to the west.

DIRECTIONS: To reach the Lost Palms Oasis Trailhead, travel almost 20 miles past Indio, heading east on I-10. Exit at the Joshua Tree National Park off ramp, turn left on the road leading into the Park and drive the 8 miles to Cottonwood Visitor Center. There you will find additional material about the National Park as well as a campground.

The best time for this hike is early spring (February to April) or October to November. It can get hot in the afternoon during those renowned warm times of year for this desert region, so bring ample supplies of cool water.

The trail begins east of the Visitor Center. You head immediately up a gradual rising slope, then pass through a series of washes. Look for the brown trail markers as you pass through the sandy washes. In spring the flowers and astonishing rich plant life will cause you to stop and enjoy the flora. As you climb, look to your rear for beautiful views of the valley and mountains surrounding this part of the park.

The trail takes you to a plateau, found at the 3 mile marker. Gaze due south for stunning vistas of the Salton Sea Basin . . . almost primeval in its rugged, wilderness look. You soon come to several small washes, out of which you climb until finally reaching the overlook for Lost Palms Oasis.

You can explore the Oasis by dropping down the indicated trail, or just admire the beauty of both the palms and the magnificent mountains to the east. This hike is unlike many others in that you feel more relaxed on a trail that has little elevation gain, feels more like a walk through a nature park and gives you an intimate feel for the mixture of rugged mountains and flowering desert found especially along the Lost Palms Oasis Trail.

Cottonwood Spring Oasis

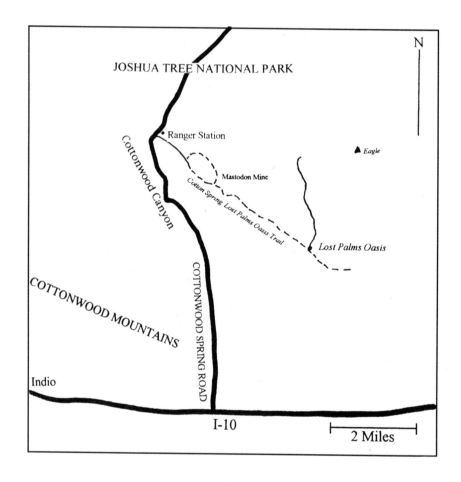

68 CAREY'S CASTLE

Length: 8 miles   **Season:** October to May
Hiking Time: 5 hours   **Information:** Joshua Tree
Elevation Gain: 1,400 feet   National Park
Difficulty: Strenuous   Cottonwood
                                   Visitor Center
                                   (619) 367-7511

Joshua Tree National Park is the home to many abandoned mines and ruins of the prospector's homes that worked them. None compare, however, to "Careys Castle." Sometime near 1940, a prospector by the name of Carey dug a mine shaft in the southern, desolate and rugged low mountains bordering Joshua Tree. He built his home (castle) under a huge boulder, as a single room shelter, and finished the front with stone work, framing a small wooden doorway. His mine is located just .25 mile west of the castle. The hike up to this ruin is adventurous, negotiating a series of beautiful canyons and dry falls, with plenty of big boulder hopping and scrambling. This hike is best taken with someone who knows the way, as no real trail exists to the "Castle."

DIRECTIONS: The adventure begins by driving on I-10 for almost 26 miles east of the Dillon Road exit in Indio. Take the Chiriaco Summit exit, turning left towards the General Patton Museum. Drive on the dirt road found between the Museum and the coffee shop (sign says RV Parking) for .5 mile until reaching the aqueduct road at the large T intersection. Turn onto this road, driving almost 3.5 miles. To your left look for a rock cairn marking a small parking area.

Head north up the wash, through desert washes and beautiful blooming flowers, cactus and occotillo in March and April.

After 1 mile take a right at the first large canyon. Hike up this canyon until reaching the first main canyon where you turn left, then left where again possible. This section lasts about 1 to 1.5 miles and includes a lot of boulder scrambling. The canyon eventually reaches another main branch. Here, take the smaller canyon to the right. You will gradually climb out of the canyon and onto the plateau area of Carey's Castle, seen as the shelter built beneath the large boulder found to the right of the canyon's end. Head west on the dirt trail for about .25 mile to see the remains of the mine shaft. Both the views and the feeling of the place are rugged, wild and captivating. Boulder flanked mountains dominate the landscape and invite further exploring.

Carey's Castle

Backcountry near Carey's Castle

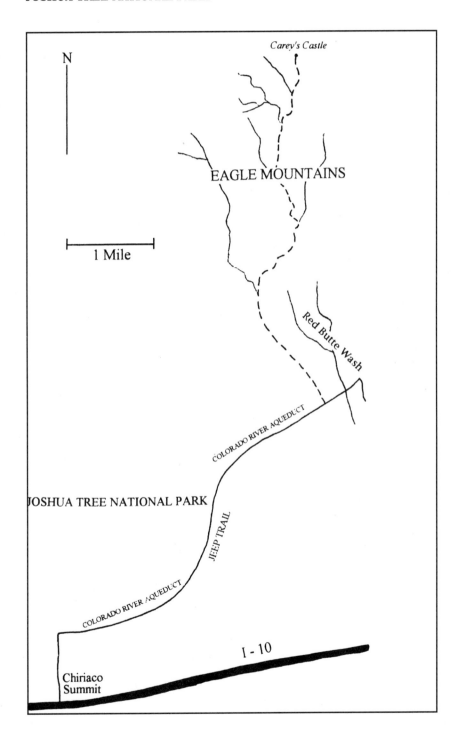

SAN GORGONIO PASS AND NEARBY

69 PIPES CANYON— PIONEERTOWN TRAIL

Length: 7 miles
Hiking Time: 4 hours
Elevation Gain: 900 feet
Difficulty: Moderate

Season: October to May
Information: BLM Office
Palm Spring
(619) 251-4800

This hike takes you from high desert up to the higher elevations in the foothills below San Gorgonio Mountain. Called Pipes Canyon due to the early rancher's efforts to bring water to the area through a pipe which was abandoned, this trail also serves equestrians. It is possible to follow the jeep road in Pipes Canyon to the Pacific Crest Trail (PCT). The PCT then continues north to Baldwin Lake Campground. The trail climbs through Joshua trees, chaparral, oak groves, with vistas below of the old western town of Pioneertown. Some rock formations in the canyon/wash are beautifully rugged and the overall effect of this hike is one of a pleasant meander into the high country.

> **DIRECTIONS:** From Palm Springs, drive west to I-10 and turn right (north) onto Hwy 62 to Yucca Valley, 22.5 miles onto Pioneertown Road. Head north/northwest through Pioneertown to Pipes Canyon Road. Turn right onto a dirt jeep road for about a mile to the gated trailhead. 4WD is recommended.

After 2.5 miles you reach a small rockhouse, beyond which the jeep road/trail has been washed away for at least a 150 foot section through a streambed. Pick up the trail and continue for another .5 mile to a large duck on the left as the canyon begins to open up. Go left up the small canyon (south) and follow the picturesque trail through an oak grove towards the saddle. Since horses use this trail, and ducks mark the way, it should be easy to follow. At 3.5 miles you are 5,280 feet in elevation—one mile up! The view of the valley is quite scenic at the top, and you can see Pioneertown in the distance.

After 5.5 miles you come to a good jeep road. Turn left and start down the road. At 6.5 miles you come to a Y. Keep heading north, following the jeep road to the rock fence and trailhead where you began.

'Mile High' on Pipes Canyon Trail

Exotic trail marker on Pipes Canyon Trail

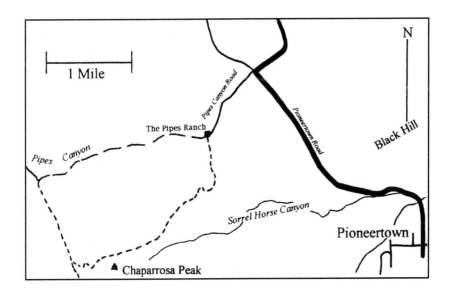

70 KITCHING CREEK TRAIL to KITCHING PEAK

Length: 10 miles
Hiking Time: 6 hours
Elevation Gain: 2,400 feet
Difficulty: Strenuous

Season: October to June
Information: USDA Forest
    Service, Mentone
    (909) 794-1123
    Wilderness
    Permit
    Required

Kitching Peak lies at the southern end of the San Bernardino Mountains and offers hikers spectacular views of the surrounding deserts, the San Gorgonio Pass below, and most especially, towering San Jacinto Mountain to the southeast. The trail travels up Millard Canyon before reaching the ridge line that will take the hiker to the summit of Kitching Peak, 6,600 feet. At times the trail can be crowded with overgrown brush and chaparral, but your real worry will be following wet winters and the infestation of flies and biting insects that can make your trip to the peak more of a jungle-like assault than a mountain adventure!

DIRECTIONS: To reach the trailhead, take I-10 two miles east of Banning and exit onto Field Road, driving north through the Morongo Indian Reservation. After 1.25 miles, turn right onto Morongo Road, where a sign indicates Millard Canyon. After .5 mile, turn left on Forest Road 2S05, that becomes a dirt road in short order. Bear a sharp right at a junction, then left at the next, until after another mile you reach your parking area just short of the creek crossing.

The trail climbs the east branch of Millard Canyon through the shade of spruce, oak and lush vegetation fed by Kitching Creek. After almost 2 miles, the trail climbs a series of switchbacks up a ridge before joining the Kitching Peak Trail, signed as Trail 2E09. 2 more miles brings you to Trail 2E24, where you will make another right, south up the tree-lined ridge before beginning your final trek up to Kitching Peak. At times this last section of trail is quite overgrown, but after coming so far, hikers do what they must to scramble to the top.

The view, especially on a clear day, is exciting and well worth the effort.

Foreground center—Kitching Peak, San Gorgonio background

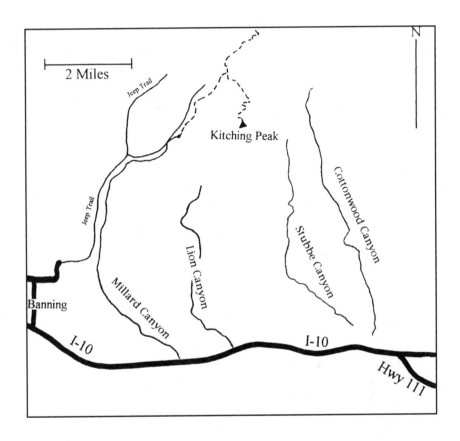

71 SAN BERNARDINO PEAK TRAIL to COLUMBINE SPRING

Length: 9 miles
Hiking Time: 5 hours
Elevation Gain: 2,100 feet
Difficulty: Strenuous

Season: June to October
Information: USDA Forest
Service, Mentone
(909) 794-1123

The San Gorgonio Wilderness has been described as an "Island of Wilderness in a Sea of Civilization," embracing over 59,000 acres of well-timbered slopes covered with sugar, limber, and Jeffrey pine, white fir, incense cedar, black and live oak, along with a generous scattering of Douglas fir. Small meadows, lakes, and the rocky slopes of the tallest mountain in Southern California, San Gorgonio Peak (11,502 feet) highlight this area of the San Bernardino Mountains. A permit is required to hike in the wilderness, and can be obtained by calling the above number.

The San Bernardino Peak Trail gives the hiker a great introduction to the many trails crisscrossing the San Bernardino Mountains, and is easily accessed from the Coachella Valley. The hike itself takes you up to 8,000 feet, affording spectacular views of the valleys below, but also shows a clear sweep of mountain ridges looking north towards Big Bear and Lake Arrowhead Lakes.

DIRECTIONS: To reach the trailhead, drive to Redlands and head north on Hwy 38. Continue to Mentone and onto the Mill Creek Ranger Station. Wilderness permits can be obtained there, but should have been called for well in advance of busy weekends. Drive 20 miles further to the town of Angelus Oaks, turn right at the fire station and look for the sign that indicates San Bernardino Peak Trail. Follow the dirt road to the small parking area, where the trail begins at the north end of the parking lot.

The trail climbs steeply up switchbacks, through forests of pine, oak and fir. As you ascend, the sharp rocky ridges across the valley assert themselves and dominate the horizon. After several miles, the trail begins to traverse a glorious plateau of manzanita and chaparral. From here, you can see the distant ridges of the northern San Bernardino Mountains.

The views continue to astound. After almost 4.5 miles you arrive at a side trail for Columbine Spring. You can continue down to the spring or hike further up the trail towards Limber Pine Bench and ultimately San Bernardino Peak (10,624 feet). The hike back down the mountain gives you the added beauty of seeing the sharp mountain ridges to the west. Take a good supply of cool water during the summer, as the lower slopes near Angeles Oaks can be quite hot.

San Gorgonio Ridge

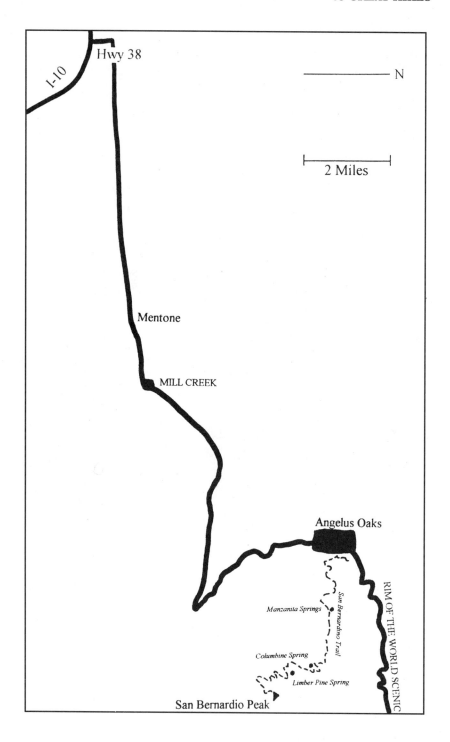

72 BIG MORONGO CANYON TRAIL

Length: 6 miles
Hiking Time: 4 hours
Elevation Loss: 1,800 feet
Difficulty: Moderate

Season: October to May
Information: BLM Office
Palm Springs
(619) 251-4800

Big Morongo Canyon Trail first shows hikers a lush riparian oasis, almost too rich in vegetation to be associated with the nearby desert, then plunges them through the wide, stream-fed wash of Big Morongo Canyon before bringing them to the desolate southern canyon northwest of Desert Hot Springs. This is best done as a shuttle hike from top to bottom, with an 1,800 foot elevation loss, gradually spread over a 6 mile stretch.

DIRECTIONS: The shuttle vehicles for the south end of the canyon need to drive on Hwy 62, north from I-10, until reaching Indian Avenue. Turn right, drive for almost a mile until coming to a dirt road to the left where you will turn and park near the chain link fence. The shuttle to the northern beginning of the trail is done by traveling up Hwy 62 for almost 10 miles, into the town of Morongo Valley and turning right at the sign indicating Big Morongo Wildlife Preserve.

After parking, begin the trail by the interpretive displays and follow the trail-road along the creek for a mile until coming to a small dam. Up to this point the trail astounds the hiker with a wetland look reminiscent of the Maryland wetlands, rather than the furthest reaches of the great Sonoran Desert. But this trail quickly empties you into the canyon proper, where you will follow a stream during the spring for almost 3 miles. Take care crossing the slippery rocks, which are often not properly anchored to the bottom. The canyon trail is really the canyon floor. You make your way as best you can, following the path of least resistance downstream, past the rock and dirt enclosed walls of Big Morongo Canyon, with flowers abundant in early springs, until the canyon ends 6 miles from where you began this adventure.

Big Morongo Preserve at trailhead

On the Big Morongo Canyon Trail

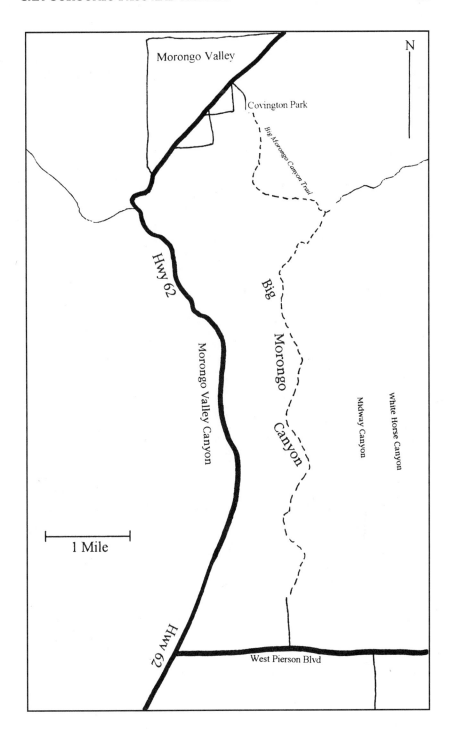

N

Morongo Valley

Covington Park

Big Morongo Canyon Trail

Hwy 62

Big

Morongo

Canyon

Morongo Valley Canyon

Midway Canyon

White Horse Canyon

1 Mile

Hwy 62

West Pierson Blvd

73 COTTONWOOD CANYON TRAIL

Length: 10 miles
Hiking Time: 6 hours
Elevation Gain: 1,800 feet
Difficulty: Strenuous

Season: October to May
Information: BLM Office
Palm Springs
(619) 251-4800

The south boundary of the San Bernardino Mountains reaches out into the San Gorgonio Pass and looks across it to the towering San Jacinto Mountains. As the San Bernardino Mountains fold out into the pass, they create some beautiful canyons that when followed, reach up into the pine-forested higher elevations. Cottonwood Canyon is one such canyon, and allows the hiker to both see into the downward sloping Coachella Valley to the east, with spectacular views of San Jacinto Mountain, as well as encounter the sylvan beauty of a cottonwood-filled canyon that empties into grassy meadows, tree-lined and cut by a beautiful mountain stream.

DIRECTIONS: To reach the trail to Cottonwood Canyon, head west 8 miles to I-10 from the Palm Springs' Indian Avenue exit to Verbenia Avenue. Turn north on Verbenia, left on Tamarack Road to Cottonwood Road. Drive north on Cottonwood for 2 miles to the Cottonwood Canyon Trailhead and parking lot. The road gets rough so a 4WD vehicle is recommended.

The obvious trail is to walk into the canyon and follow it to the end. This, however, is too rugged a bushwhack. You encounter steep waterfalls where ladders help you negotiate up and over. The trail forces you to hack your way through thickets of underbrush and trees. The more "sane" route is to head north from the parking lot, across a flat stretch leading to the low hills on the right side of the canyon. Climb up this right side for several hundred feet (quite steep) until you find the trail at the top. Several false trails lead from this main trail, but eventually all trails feed into the main trail. Once on this main trail, follow it up the ridge as it meanders sometimes beneath it, sometimes on it, with great views of the lower deserts and San Jacinto Mountain.

After 3 miles or so you will begin to appreciate the view down into Cottonwood Canyon. In late fall, the cottonwoods are brilliant yellow, while turning a delicious apple-green in spring. The trail eventually leads you down into the canyon, along a stream, and into the high country, a lush contrast to the desert you began in.

This trail continues for several more miles, but most hikers find the stream and meadowland woods too tempting a lunch-and-turn-around spot. On the way back, be careful to note the proper trail turns, as some false trails lead east from the top of the ridge. You should mark them yourself with cairns on the way up canyon. The views are marvelous and dominate your vision all the way to the trailhead.

Cottonwood Canyon Trailhead

74 PACIFIC CREST TRAIL NORTH from I-10

Length: 10 miles
Hiking Time: 5 hours
Elevation Gain: 1,500 feet
Difficulty: Moderate

Season: October to May
Information: BLM Office
            Palm Springs
            (619) 251-4800

The Pacific Crest Trail (PCT) enters the environs of the Coachella Valley south of Hwy 74 in Garner Valley, threads up to the Desert Divide ridge overlooking the desert, travels along the San Jacinto Mountains west to Idyllwild, cuts down the north slope of San Jacinto Mountain and spills across the San Gorgonio Pass over I-10, before beginning its ascent up the San Bernardino Mountains and into the Big Bear Lake area. The small section of the PCT that leaves I-10 to head north is a modest hike, considering the spectacular countryside it traversed along the 70 miles from Hwy 74, but makes a good moderate hike in early spring, where wildflowers and blooming cactus ascent the trail.

DIRECTIONS: To pick up the PCT north, head west 8 miles from the Indian Avenue exit in Palm Springs to Verbenia Avenue. Turn north on Verbenia, left on Tamarack Road, heading west to Fremontia Road. Fifty yards west of the sign post on the right side of the road, the PCT starts through fields of brittle bush and a wash. You find a well-marked trail leading up to the Cottonwood Canyon Trail sign post and parking lot. The PCT leaves the parking lot at the NW corner, goes over a creek and makes for the low hills nearby.

From here the trail is a meander, climbing over low hills for miles, giving you views of the higher elevations that it will eventually reach. Hikers should explore this "quiet" section of the trail for as far as comfortable, before turning back.

Pacific Crest Trail
north from I-10

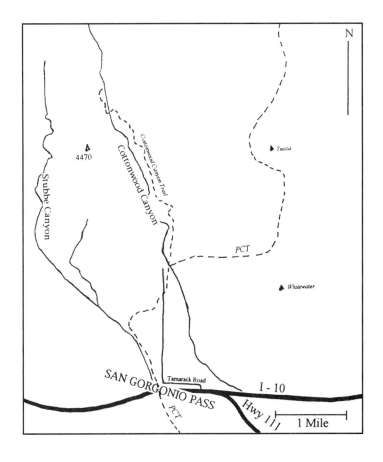

75 PACIFIC CREST TRAIL SOUTH
from I-10

Length: 10 miles
Hiking Time: 5 hours
Elevation Gain: 2,000 feet
Difficulty: Strenuous

Season: October to May
Information: BLM Office
Palm Springs
(619) 251-4800

The Pacific Crest Trail (PCT) comes down the north face of San Jacinto Mountain, spilling over into the San Gorgonio Pass, across I-10 and north-ward up the slopes of the San Bernardino Mountains. The easiest access to this section of the PCT is from I-10, where you cross the flat desert before reaching the low foothills of San Jacinto Mountain and eventually the higher elevations at 9,000 feet above Snow Creek Canyon.

> **DIRECTIONS:** To reach the trailhead, drive west on I-10 for 8 miles from the Indian Avenue exit. Turn north onto Verbenia Avenue, left on Tamarack Road to Fremontia Road. The PCT starts 50 yards from the sign post, on the left side of the road.

Head south under the I-10 bridges where you come out into a large wash. Veer southeast towards the high voltage lines. You may begin see-ing the brown PCT trail markers, providing the spring rains have not washed them away. Head to the second last high voltage tower from the mountainside. You will then pick up the PCT markers leading to the paved Snow Creek Road. Turn right onto Falls Creek Road to the gated lands of the Water District. Follow the paved road up 2 miles to the PCT marker on the right side of the road.

From here, the trail begins climbing the mountain, making steep switchbacks for nearly 16 miles to the top, where it connects with the trail systems around San Jacinto Peak. The views are spectacular, but unfortunately, this section of trail is too long for a casual day hike, and needs to be done as part of a 2- to 3-day backpack.

Snow capped Mount San Jacinto from Pacific Crest Trailhead

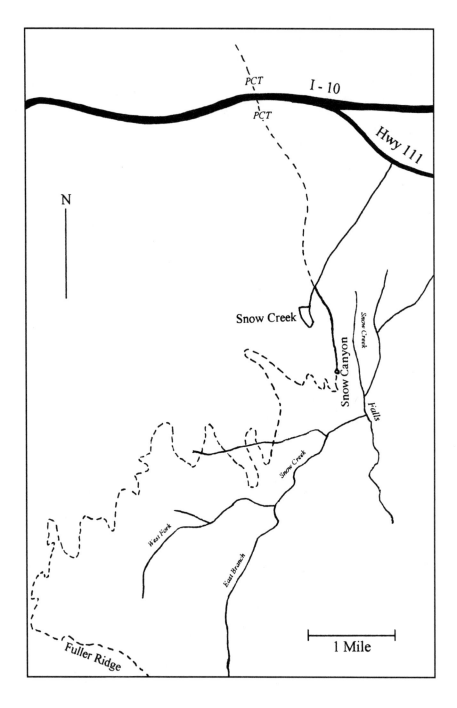

Appendix:
Hikes According to Difficulty

EASY HIKES

miles

5	The Painted Canyon/Ladder Canyon Loop
5	Horsethief Creek via Cactus Spring Trail
6	The Pushawalla Palms and Canyon Trail
3	Willis Palms and West Mesa Trail
6	Coachella Valley Preserve Trails
5	The Ernie Maxwell Scenic Trail
2	San Andreas Canyon
4	Earl Henderson Trail
3	Santa Rosa Mountain Road to Toro Peak
1.5	Barker Dam Loop
3	Hurkey Creek Trail

MODERATE HIKES

miles

5	Box Canyon's Cave Hike "The Grottos"
4–6	Carrizo Canyon
9	Cactus Spring Trail
7	Jo Pond Trail to Cedar Spring
9	Jo Pond Trail to Fobes Saddle Overlook
6	Eisenhower Peak Loop
5	Devil's Slide Trail to Saddle Junction
6	Murray Canyon Trail
8–10	Palm Canyon Trail to Little Paradise

8	Palm Canyon Trail to Bullseye Rock
9	North and South Lykken Trail
2	The Palm Springs Desert Museum Trail
6	Big Morongo Canyon Trail
4	Ryan Mountain Trail
8	Lost Palms Oasis Trail at Cottonwood Spring
8	Lost Horse Mine Loop
7	Shannon Trail Loop
6	The Araby Trail
10	Pacific Crest Trail North from I-10
6	The Schey Trail
6	Covington Loop Trail
7	Pipes Canyon—Pioneertown Trail

STRENUOUS HIKES

miles

8	Bear Creek Canyon Ridge
10	Lost Canyon via Boo Hoff Trail
12	The Boo Hoff Trail to La Quinta
16	Art Smith Trail
6	Magnesia Falls Canyon
18	Agua Alta Spring
8	Sawmill Road Trail
16	Palm Canyon Pines-to-Palms Trail
11	South Fork of the Pacific Crest Trail (PCT)
14	North Fork of the PCT to Live Oak Spring
6	Fobes Saddle to Spitler Peak and Apache Spring
12	The Zen Center to Red Tahquitz Overlook
10	Spitler Peak Trail
7	South Ridge Trail to Tahquitz Peak Overlook
13	Devil's Slide Trail to Tahquitz Peak Lookout Loop
10	Devil's Slide Trail to Laws Junction
11	Devil's Slide Trail to Red Tahquitz Overlook
11	Ramona Trail to Tool Box Spring
12	Deer Springs Trail to Saddle Junction/Humber Park

11	Palm Springs Aerial Tramway to San Jacinto Peak
12	Palm Springs Aerial Tramway to Saddle Junction Loop
6.5	Seven Pines Trail to Marion Mountain Camp
15	Fuller Ridge Trail to San Jacinto Peak
7	Black Mountain Trail
4	Palm Canyon Trail to the Right Fork
10	Maynard Mine Trail
10	The West Fork Trail to San Andreas Canyon
10	Kitching Creek Trail to Kitching Peak
12	Long Canyon to Chuckawalla Bill's Ruins
9	San Bernardino Peak Trail to Columbine Spring
10	Eureka Peak Loop
8	Carey's Castle
10	Fern Canyon
10	Murray Hill (Peak)
16	The Hahn-Buena Vista Trail
14	Humber Park—Devil's Slide Trail to Caramba Overlook
10	Cottonwood Canyon Trail
10	Pacific Crest Trail South from I-10
15	Guadalupe Trail to Sugarloaf Cafe
22	"Cactus to Clouds" Hike
16	Rockhouse Canyon Trail
13	Jo Pond/Cedar Spring Trail to Palm Canyon Trading Post

About the Authors

Philip Ferranti has hiked the Western United States for over 20 years. He has spent much of that time exploring the trails in and near the Coachella Valley/Palm Springs area. During the summer Philip hikes out of Boulder, Colorado, with the Colorado Mountain Club. Inspired by their organization, he founded the Coachella Valley Hiking Club in 1992 and has guided it to becoming the fastest growing hiking club in the United States. He has written for Backpacker magazine and contributes to hiking columns for local newspapers. He also does Career Counseling for College of the Desert and Palm Springs Unified School District. As president of Transformation Seminars since 1981, Philip specializes in Stress Management seminars and believes that hiking is the ultimate and most enjoyable stress management program.

Bruce and Denice Hagerman have recently retired from their successful RV Business. They began hiking on Vancouver Island, British Columbia in 1981. Their love of hiking has taken them to forty of the states and all of Canada's ten provinces. They are founding members and hike leaders of the Coachella Valley Hiking Club and have spent the last three winters devoted to exploring and enjoying the fabulous hikes found in and near the Coachella Valley/Palm Springs area. As team members of Palm Desert Sheriff Search and Rescue they utilize their knowledge of hiking and of this area in the searches.

FOR ADDITIONAL COPIES OF:

75 GREAT HIKES in and near PALM SPRINGS and the COACHELLA VALLEY

KENDALL/HUNT PUBLISHING COMPANY
4050 Westmark Drive
P. O. Box 1840
Dubuque, Iowa 52004-1840
     Phone: 1-800-228-0810   *Fax: 1-800-772-9165*

MEMBERSHIP APPLICATION

I hereby apply for membership in the Coachella Valley Hiking Club (CVHC). I agree to be solely responsible for my own safety and to take every precaution to provide for my own safety and well-being while participating in activities of the CVHC.

- Individual membership $25.00 annual dues
- Family membership $35.00 annual dues

Please make all checks payable to CVHC. Send application and check to CVHC, P.O. Box 10750, Palm Desert, CA 92255.

PRINT OR TYPE

Last Name   _____

First Name   _____

Last Name (Family Member) _____

First Name (Family Member)_____

Last Name (Family Member) _____

First Name (Family Member)_____

Last Name (Family Member) _____

First Name (Family Member)_____

Street Address_____

Apt. No. _____ City _____

State _____ Zip _____

Home Phone Number_____

Best Time to Call _____